D1070230

PSYCHOMETRIC ANALYSIS

BY

MAX FREEDOM LONG

AUTHOR OF

The Secret Science Behind Miracles
The Secret Science At Work
Growing Into Light
Self-Suggestion

◆

DeVorss & Co., *Publishers*
P.O. Box 550
Marina Del Rey, Ca. 90291

COPYRIGHT 1959, BY

Huna Research Publications

All rights reserved. No part of this book may be reproduced
in any form without the written permission of the publisher.

ISBN: 0-87516-045-X

Printed in the United States of America by
BOOK GRAPHICS, INC.
Marina del Rey, CA 90291

CONTENTS

INTRODUCTION

Shortly after my first book on the recovery of the ancient Huna system was published in America, there was organized an experimental group to test the old beliefs and practices. This was the "Huna Research Associates". Members were scattered around the world, and most of the research was carried out by individuals who took on assigned work and who reported to me by letter from time to time.

In order to keep all of the members in touch and advised of the work in hand and of the results obtained, the HRA Bulletin was issued at frequent intervals.

Many of the experimental and research projects were related only indirectly to the Huna Practices of other years. However, all of them were of such a nature that re-examination in the light of Huna theories offered the best hope of a more complete understanding.

When the HRA Bulletins were discontinued late in the year 1957, some of the most valuable work units were still unfinished. As the research continued under my supervision, and as much new information was collected and projects were brought as near to completion as possible, there was need for a final ordering of materials and a fresh presentation of the problems involved and of the conclusions reached in trying to solve them.

For that reason, this proposed series of small books might well be considered a rounding out of the unfinished business of the HRA.

One project which was reported briefly in my second book, "The Secret Science At Work", aroused much interest. It was the study of a method of measuring the characteristics and intelligence of people by means of an instrument which had been invented by Dr. Oscar Brunler. He had based his work on the earlier experiments of a Frenchman, M. Bovis. The instrument was called, "The Brunler-Bovis Biometer".

The value of such an instrument was immediately apparent. Some of Dr. Brunler's lectures and brief writings were reported verbatim in the HRA Bulletin from time to time. A few of the HRAs, including myself, were privileged to learn to make readings on one of the few instruments which had been constructed. But standing in the way of more general testing and research was the fact that the instruments were not available for purchase.

The failure to manufacture and market Biometers on a commercial scale appears to have been caused by a combination of circumstances, not least of which was the fear that the instrument might be mistaken for one of the "radionics" machines used for the diagnosis and treatment of disease by some physicians, but not allowed, under federal law, to be made and sold in interstate trade.

It so happened that the "radiations" which the "radionics" instruments were supposed to pick up from a patient during diagnosis were never proven to exist.

Unfortunately, the Biometer lacked a sound explanation of just what it registered. Dr. Brunler was accustomed to say that it picked up "brain radiations" and analyzed them, but he hastened to explain that these radiations were not of the usual electrical type, being "dielectric" in nature.

There was also secrecy concerning a supposed assembly of component parts said to be sealed in the base of the instrument.

In any event, the lack of Biometers for experimental use on the part of the members of the HRA hampered investigation of the important things which it was evident the instrument could do. Lacking the information needed to construct an instrument of the Brunler sort, the best that could be done was to find one of the old French Biometers formerly manufactured by M. Bovis, and start with it to try to reconstruct the steps taken by Dr. Brunler in improving it. At the same time, it was necessary to try to find a more convincing explanation of how and why the instruments did what they were known to do.

Dr. Brunler died in 1952. While the theories he had tentatively advanced were slowly being replaced, nothing was ever taken from the stature of his genius which was displayed in the invention of his version of the Biometer and his monumental work of dividing the reading procedure into three parts, then discovering the significance of the indications given through the instrument readings.

For the reader who comes to this book without a knowledge of Huna such as may be derived from the reading of my earlier books, it has been found necessary to include a brief explanation of parts of the Huna theory (to be found in my basic book, "The Secret Science Behind Miracles") in order to make clear the things written about the Biometric system. It has also been necessary to give a short résumé of

3

the work done by Dr. Brunler in developing the system.

It is hoped that those already familiar with the books and the HRA Bulletins will accept this fresh presentation as a good review in preparation for the setting forth of a considerable amount of information not to be found elsewhere.

MAX FREEDOM LONG

Chapter 1
What Is Psychometry?

As the experimental work with the Biometer progressed, especially in the years following Dr. Oscar Brunler's death, so many changes were made in the theories covering the working of the instrument that a new and more acceptable name for the system was needed to apply to the changed system after it was reshaped to include the explanations offered by Huna.

The name, "Psychometric Analysis", was selected for general use, but the full name for the process would be, "Psychometric Analysis of Human Character and Mentality".

"Psychometry" is a word coined some years ago in psychical research circles. It means the measuring or analysis of something without the use of the usual physical means. The use of the five senses is barred. Even distance and time are pushed aside as physical things.

When a psychometric reading is to be made, it is the custom to hand the reader some object that has at one time or another been in contact with the thing or person who is to be the subject of the psychic investigation. Writing done with pen and ink, especially signatures, as well as photographs and objects long worn or carried by the subject, direct the reader in making the contact with people, living or dead, near at hand or at a distance. Objects, such as a fragment of lava from a volcano or a tooth from a mastodon, furnish the means of making the psychic contact where persons are not involved.

In an article on page 317 of his "Encyclopedia of Psychic Science", Dr. Nandor Fodor tells of the famous experiments carried on between the years of 1853 and 1863 by Prof. William Denton, of Boston:

"On examining the fragment of a mastodon tooth, Mrs. Denton (who was doing the reading) said: 'My impression is that it is a part of some monstrous animal, probably part of a tooth. I feel like a perfect monster, with heavy legs, unwieldy head, and a very large body. I go down to a shallow stream to drink. I can hardly speak, my jaws are so heavy. I feel like getting down on all fours. What a noise comes through the wood. I have an impulse to answer it. My ears are very large and leathery, and I can almost fancy they flap my face as I move my head. There are some older ones than I. It seems, too, so out of keeping to be talking with these heavy jaws. They are dark brown, as if they had been completely tanned. There is one old fellow with large tusks, that looks very tough. I see several young ones; in fact, there is a whole herd. '"

Later on in the article we read: "Apparently a very slight contact (with an object) will suffice to impart such a personal influence (as will allow the contact to be made by the reader). William Stead cut pieces of blank paper from the bottom pages of letters of eminent people, just below the signature of each, and sent them to Miss Ross, marked No. 1. Lady, No. 2. Gentleman. The readings were very successful....."

Readings made psychometrically from objects owned by individuals or from their signatures, give the appearance and situation of the individual very

6

often, as well as impressions concerning the character, mentality and general goodness or badness. In many well-documented cases, readings have been made in which the persons were unknown to the readers, but who were described as criminals, when such they were.

The difference between psychometry, as it has just been described, and the use of the Biometer or of Psychometric Analysis (in which only the pendulum and a set of artificial measuring standards are used) is primarily one of the scope of a reading.

In Psychometry, scenes of the past may be re-enacted, and personal appearance of the subject noted. In Psychometric Analysis, on the other hand, no visual or auditory impressions are received. There are no sensations, no identification of the reader with the subject of the reading. All that is to be seen is the swinging of a pendulum as its action denotes on a chart the three things to be measured in the subject at the moment: his character as it is grounded in his conscious and subconscious parts of mind, and the over-all intelligence of the mind as a whole.

From this brief explanation it will be seen why the term "Biometer" has been dropped and "Psychometric Analysis" adopted. For convenience, the initials "P.A." are used, just as in mentioning "Extra Sensory Perception" we have come to use the initials E.S.P. Or, as we have shortened "Intelligence Quotient" to I. Q.

. . . .

Just to look at a child or adult, or to listen to what he may say, has given a very poor indication of the character or mental development of the individual. For almost a hundred years we have been trying to invent tests which will give an accurate estimate of the goodness or badness natural to the ones tested. We wish to learn something of their character and to be able to classify them as generally destructive or constructive in their approach to life. We also wish to ascertain by testing the degree of intelligence with which the person may have been blessed at birth. Furthermore, we wish to learn if possible whether there is natural skill in the hands, or in the use of some of the five senses.

The result of the efforts to invent workable tests has been a fair one. But the usual "Intelligence Quotient" tests still leave much to be desired. Most of them depend upon the answers given to a set of questions. This allows for deception on the part of the one tested. The ability to reason, or to use certain natural manual skills may be tested by observing the time taken to fit appropriately shaped blocks into corresponding holes cut in a board. In such tests the age and experience of the subject must be taken into account in arriving at the figure to represent the I. Q.

The naturally bad or destructive child may pretend goodness and give glib answers to questions of correct manners, morals or conduct. On the other hand, a naturally good and constructive child who has had faulty rearing, may give a most confusing and misleading set of answers to the same questions.

In testing to find mental defects, the difficulties multiply rapidly once one is beyond the simpler sets of questions. Imaginings aroused by the contemplation of an ink blot, may or may not reflect hidden fixations or obsessions.

Many forms of mental irregularity have come to

be blamed on the "subconscious", but this "part of the mind" is still very poorly understood despite the recent addition to this field of knowledge through the rediscovery of the ancient Huna system of psychology and psychic science. The possibility that the living may be influenced for good or evil by the spirits of the dead is still steadfastly denied in medical and psychiatric circles even though all symptoms point to obsession in a large portion of the neurotic or insane.

The present status of the testing art in question is stalemate. Little of value has been added to the methods in over a decade. The field is crying for a chance to be plowed up anew and replanted.

The new methodology of Psychometric Analysis is, as has been said, based on the original work of M. Bovis and the later changes and innovations made by Dr. Oscar Brunler. To these were added fresh data drawn from Psychic Science, and an almost completely new and different set of explanatory theories derived from the ancient Huna system.

The end result is a valuable addition to the older test methods used to arrive at the I.Q. and a general assessment of the nature and capacity of the individual.

In using the P.A. method, the operation is not in any way dependent upon answers given by the one being tested. No fitting of blocks into holes is needed. There is no looking at ink blots. Because of this a whole series of chances to make errors becomes eliminated.

Another great advantage of the P.A. system is that a reading can be taken successfully of a child a few weeks after its birth instead of waiting until the age of six years or more.

Anxious parents can learn at once what to expect of a child and can have guidance from the P.A. information to help them to rear the child, plan his schooling, and, in due time, to help him to decide upon a life work suited to his ability and tailored to compensate for his lacks and defects.

A still further advantage of the use of the P.A. system is that the subject cannot at any age, old or young, cover up his natural leaning to goodness or to badness—toward being constructive or destructive. There is also a strange mixture of goodness and badness which the P.A. reading can indicate. Furthermore, the reading can show defects in the "will" of the subject. And, last, but not less important, the presence of blocks or fixations in the subconscious are located, and obsessional vulnerability warned of in advance.

Unlike the indirect measuring method of the ink blot tests, the P.A. method measures the "self" of the subject only after dividing it into the "conscious" and "subconscious" parts. Each part is tested by itself and in terms of its own characteristics.

The active "will" and the reasoning power come under the heading of things to be learned about the "conscious mind" self. (Called the "middle self" in Huna, as distinct from the "subconscious" or "low" self.) The subjective "will" and the memory are assigned to the second part of the "self". (For the sake of easier presentation, let us now use the Huna term.)

The faulty "will" of the middle self of a subject makes concentration on thoughts or work difficult. As the middle self "will" exerts control over the

10

instinctive or animal "will" of the low self, any defect in the controlling "will" allows the low self to get out of hand.

If a child is given his P.A. and is found to be lacking in some way, training can begin at once to try to compensate for the defect, be it one of the "will" of the middle self or of the "personality" of the low self. The progress of correction can be checked with ease and accuracy, month by month and year by year.

In adult life the individual can work to perfect his various qualities and can be checked as often as necessary to determine the degree of success or of failure.

More will be said later about the many additional benefits to society in general which will be made possible if P.A. can be introduced, operators trained, and the new system brought to acceptance and extensive use in all departments of human endeavor.

Chapter 2
BOVIS, BRUNLER, AND THE BIOMETER

The story of the development of the Biometer is a most interesting one. It will bear retelling for the benefit of the reader who has not become familiar with it as part of the earlier work of the Huna Research Associates.

Some years before Dr. Joseph B. Rhine began his famous investigation of ESP at Duke University in the United States, there developed a great wave of interest in the pendulum in Europe. This was especially strong in France, and in that country an obscure man named Bovis discovered that, with the aid of a pendulum, he could lay a hand on a cheese or a cask of wine and be told by his subconscious self via the agreed-upon movements given to the pendulum, whether the cheese or wine was good or bad.

Bovis seems to have been a professional tester at a time when samples had to be taken of such things as cheeses or wines and tasted to determine their quality. This was a slow and expensive method. But Bovis appears to have proved to the satisfaction of his employers that his method was workable, even if he failed to convince them that his explanation of what he had discovered was correct.

In an effort to find a method of determining the degree of goodness or its lack in things to be tested, and perhaps to try to give at least an outward appearance of scientific basis, M. Bovis invented a small instrument for testing which he named the

THE ORIGINAL BOVIS "BIOMETER". (1/3 size.)

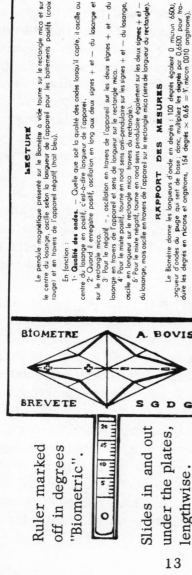

MICA –1+

LECTURE

Le pendule magnétique présenté sur le Biomètre à vide tourne sur le rectangle mica et sur le centre du losange, oscille selon la longueur de l'appareil pour les battements positifs (croix rouge) et en travers de l'appareil négatif (trait bleu).

En fonction :

1° **Qualité des ondes.** — Quelle que soit la qualité des ondes lorsqu'il capte, il oscille au centre du losange en positif; c'est-à-dire longueur de l'appareil.

2° Quand il enregistre positif, oscillation en long aux deux signes + et – du losange et sur le rectangle mica.

3° Pour le négatif –, oscillation en travers de l'appareil sur les deux signes + et – du losange en travers de l'appareil et sens de longueur sur le rectangle mica.

4° Pour le mixte positif, tourne en rond sens anti-pendulaire sur les signes + et – du losange, oscille en longueur sur le rectangle mica travers du rectangle).

5° Pour le mixte négatif, tourne en rond sens pendulaire également sur les deux signes + et – du losange, mais oscille en travers de l'appareil sur le rectangle mica (sens de longueur du rectangle).

RAPPORT DES MESURES

Le Biomètre donne les longueurs d'onde en degrés : 100 degrés égalent 0 micron 650U, ongueur d'ondes du puge qui sert de base: donc, multipliez les degrés par 0,6500 pour traduire les degrés en microns et angstroms, 154 degrés × 0,65 = 1° micron 0010 angstroms).

BIOMETRE   A. BOVIS

BREVETE   S G D G

Ruler marked off in degrees "Biometric".

Slides in and out under the plates, lengthwise.

Iron plate with cover of paper on which the design or "diamond" was printed.

The mica plate lay under the printed paper cover at this end of the Bovis Biometer.

The circle at the left end of the ruler shows where the cup for the "sample" was to be placed. The pendulum is not shown, although Bovis manufactured them for sale.

"Biometer". It consisted of a pendulum plus a small measuring stick marked off in "Degrees Biometric", which he arbitrarily elected to make about two centimeters in length. In his literature he declared that all things threw off waves, and that with his instrument the waves were measured and their length ascertained. He even went so far as to say that the new "degree biometric" could be changed to angstrom units by multiplying it by a certain number. In this way he managed to hint strongly that his "waves" were similar to those of light. He even painted his instrument dark red on the wooden parts, saying that this matched the lower wave lengths of light and did something or other to make his instrument work more accurately.

In addition to the small measuring ruler, he included in his instrument two small plates, one of iron and one of mica. The ruler was made to slide back and forth under the two plates from the left, and the iron plate was the first one under which the ruler passed when pushed inward.

Readings or testings were made by placing a small sample of the thing to be tested in a cup at the zero end of the ruler, or he may have connected the cup with a cheese or cask of wine by a wire or thread as was done by later experimenters who got good results even if they did violence to the "length of the waves" theory.

Readings began by holding the pendulum over one of the plates after another. If a clockwise swing of the pendulum took place over the iron plate as well as over the one made of mica, a perfect cheese or other item was indicated. But if a counterclockwise swing came over the mica plate, then there was a lack of

14

perfection indicated, and a third part of the reading was in order. The pendulum was again held over the metal plate but the sample on its cup was moved with the entire ruler closer and closer to the plate, the free end of the ruler sliding gradually under the iron plate and stopping its slide only when the pendulum began to swing over the plate as between the hours of 12 and 6 o'clock had the plate been a clock face.

This arbitrary "convention" allowed the subconscious self to indicate by the swing when the reading on the ruler was correct for the thing tested. If the degree which was marked on the ruler just at the edge of the plate was read, it became the indicator of the goodness or badness of the cheese. There were 100 degrees on the ruler, and if it read 70 degrees at the point where the ruler disappeared under the left edge of the iron plate, the reading indicated the fact that the cheese was only 70% perfect.

In time Bovis began measuring the health of his acquaintances by having them place a thumb on the cup to serve as a "sample" of themselves. In no long time he was diagnosing the health of people in terms of percentages of perfection.

Later on he invented several instruments with which to make more definite readings of things like the heart or liver or lungs of those read. The demand for the instruments soon became such that he manufactured and sold them, furnishing booklets to instruct buyers in their use and the theory behind them, his "wave" theory, of course.

An important addition to the idea of placing the thumb in or on the cup of the ruler soon developed. Whether M. Bovis was responsible for this or not is uncertain, but it came about that a dull needle was tied to the end of a cord attached at the other end to the ruler of the Biometer. Then the end of the needle was pressed against different points on the palm and fingers of the patient's hand, each of some dozen or more points being said to represent some organ or tissue of the body, and a reading of the condition of the organ or tissue, as an isolated part, thus made possible.

This needle and cord matter bore interesting fruit eventually. While M. Bovis was still alive, and at some time after World War I, Dr. Oscar Brunler entered the picture. He was a physicist and engineer rather than a physician. He was known for the invention of a flame that would burn under water and cut metal so that it had been a great help in salvaging sunken ships. He was also a designer of oil refineries in which a naked flame burns in the midst of the crude oil to heat it directly. He was a man of very great curiosity as well as of endless interests. When he heard of the Biometer, he called on M. Bovis in France and purchased an instrument.

He had already become interested in the dowsing rod and had learned to use one to locate water or minerals. In a very short time he had mastered the use of the Biometer.

As Dr. Brunler related his story at a much later date, when he had come to the United States and had begun to lecture and to make readings with his version of the Biometer, he had, in London, made a discovery of great significance and had followed it with much testing. He found that the Biometer could be used to measure the brain waves and character to give a Biometric reading of the status of what he called "the place in evolution of the soul."

He had found that there was a place on the very tip of the thumb which, when touched with the needle, would give a contact with the brain, and so of the intelligence, of the subject being measured. He soon developed a method by which the reading could be divided into three separate parts or readings, one for the "will" of the conscious mind, one for the "will" or "character" of the subconscious part of mind, and one for the intelligence of the subject. Some time later his findings were described in lectures, and the lectures were printed in booklet form in Washington, D.C., and in Los Angeles, Calif.

The basic things in Psychometric Analysis were nearly all worked out by Dr. Brunler and given to the world in his lectures and writings as well as his continual demonstration of the method by use of his improved instrument which he called, "The Brunler-Bovis Biometer". His instrument differed from that of Bovis mainly in taking the mica plate from the right of the iron plate. (Brass and other metals were also used to replace the iron plate.) Because of the far greater length of the ruler, he did not try to slide it under the metal plate as a reading progressed. Instead, he arranged to have the tip of the subject's thumb drawn slowly away from the plate while the pendulum was being swung, and when the pendulum motion indicated that the proper distance from the plate to the thumb tip had been reached, a reading of the number of degrees on the ruler where the thumb had stopped was made.

Instead of the tip of the subject's thumb, the needle and thread method could be used. For this a metal band was placed around the subject's head and a conductor of the waves, in the form of a cord or insulated wire, was run out from the head band and attached to a cup which was fastened to a small wooden block. This could be slid back and forth along the metal ruler until the correct point for the reading was reached.

The Bovis theory of radiating waves of various lengths being sent out by the thing or person tested, was changed during this period so that the waves were described as being "dielectric" or a negative form of electricity. Of course, this made no sense to the electrical engineers who attempted to find out what the Biometer actually measured. Dr. Brunler undoubtedly knew the fallacy of the explanation, but, having nothing exact to offer, he allowed it to stand. Toward the end of his life he became well acquainted with the Huna theory and explanation of the mechanism, but did not endorse it publicly, possibly because to do so would have demanded too much profitless effort in making the retractions and giving the new explanation. (After his death, his widow and very able collaborator, Dr. Grace Brunler, continued with lectures and with teaching the use of the Biometer, making no changes in either the theory of the method or in the instrument.)

Disregarding the question of the validity of the wave theory, it can be stated without danger of contradiction that the ruler, plate and pendulum of the Brunler-Bovis type of instrument supply an excellent device with which to train the low self to become proficient in making P.A. tests and reporting them through the sign language or "convention" of which the pendulum is the "voice".

So well did Dr. Brunler explore the possible meanings of the things reported through the pendulum by the low self, that few additions have been made to his compilations. He will always be looked upon as the discoverer of most of the basic things upon which the system of Psychometric Analysis has been built.

Chapter 3
Basic Huna Beliefs and Psychometry

It has become evident that the entire Biometric system of measuring is based on Psychometry. As Huna offers the only complete and rationally acceptable set of theories to explain the mechanics of Psychometry, it must be described.

The Huna system of beliefs and practices is very old. It was known in Egypt and India at a very early time, and was carried many centuries ago to Polynesia. There it was preserved for more centuries by the native priests, or kahunas.

The last fully initiated Huna priests died in the late years of the last century, outlawed by the rulers, dominated by the missionaries. They had been unable to find in the younger generation of their day candidates willing to undergo the long training to become priests of the highest order, especially as they would have to practice their healing art in hiding.

The lore had always been kept secret, and when the last of the great kahunas was gone, Huna became lost to the world. Fortunately, the fact that there had existed such a secret lore, and that it was of the greatest value, led to an effort to learn what the "Secret" had been and to reconstruct it.

Three men worked on the project, and in 1936 the writer was able to describe the system in part in a book. Research continued and more books followed. By now the system is fairly well understood.

For those readers who will accept the Huna explanations, at least as a working hypothesis, we give here a very brief outline of the ten basic beliefs of Huna, then go on to explain in terms of the elements represented by the beliefs how Psychometry works from a physio-mechanical angle.

* * *

Huna considers man to be composed of what, in the terms of modern psychology and occultism, may be called three "selves" or spirits, the subconscious, or low self, the conscious, or middle self, and the superconscious, or High Self. These three selves are separate and individual, but work together as a team to make up the man.

Each of the three selves has an "astral body" or "double". During physical life, these invisible bodies either interpenetrate the physical body, or, as in the case of the High Self and its tenuous body, may usually remain at a distance from the physical structure but connected to it with a "silver cord" of invisible substance.

Each of the three selves is at a different stage of upward evolution, with the High Self the most advanced. Each has its own special way of thinking as well as its own talents. Each has its own way of using the vital force which is manufactured in the physical body by the low self for the use of all three.

The three spirits live in their invisible bodies after the death of the physical body. In Huna these invisible bodies have been known as the "Shadowy bodies" from at least the time of the early dynasties of ancient Egypt.

The shadowy body (*kino aka*, in the Hawaiian tongue), is best described by saying that it is made

21

of what, in Psychic Science, we have come to call invisible ectoplasmic substance. This substance has two very peculiar characteristics. First, it can be stretched out into an invisible, microscopic thread miles and miles long. Second, it can conduct a flow of vital force as a wire conducts electricity, and on the flow can carry thought forms embodying sensory or mental impressions.

Huna has a symbol for almost all of the elements which we have been mentioning as part of its general lore. The shadowy threads are symbolized by the strands of a spider's web. The low self is likened to a spider who sits at the center of a web of threads or strands which radiate outward in all directions and connect the spider with all things which it has at one time or another touched. Each touch has caused a thread of the web material to stick to the thing or person contacted and to connect it or him with the symbolical spider (with the low self).

This is all very complicated when told in so few words, but an example of the use of the mechanism will help to make it more easily understood.

The reader who makes a Psychometric Analysis of another person may be likened to a man using a trained spider. The spider is, of course, his low self. It has the ability to project a part of its consciousness out along any shadowy thread which it may discover, and go instantly and invisibly to the far end of the thread. In making a reading, a signature may be used.

All signatures, when written in ink, have connected to them as they are written, a thread of the kind under discussion. As such threads last for a very long time, any reader who may look at a sig-

22

nature with the intention of making a P.A. of the writer, will have a means of getting into contact with him.

The low self of the reader simply projects a part of its consciousness and vital force along the connecting thread, finds the writer, studies him, and then withdraws from the thread, carrying back to the body of the reader the information desired.

Once the information is acquired, it is passed on to the waiting middle self of the reader by means of the pendulum and the scale and chart of the Biometer.

The low self, and it only, can spin shadowy threads or follow those spun by others and attached to such things as signatures. For this reason, it is the only one of the three selves who can perform the feat of sending or receiving telepathic messages. (Such messages are composed of thought forms sent back and forth between persons on connecting threads of the shadowy substance.)

Other than the Huna explanation of the mechanics of Psychometry, we have little of value. Psychical Research has, during the past century, verified the genuineness of Psychometry and of such things as mind reading, telepathy, ESP and the phenomena of apporting and materialization. But, while there has been left no reasonable doubt that such things are real, no equally acceptable explanation has been offered to tell how and why these things come about.

Two tentative explanations have been offered, but neither is adequate. The first theory is that the spirits of the dead perform all the work of making a psychometric reading. This would make of the one doing the reading a medium whose first task would be to call the spirits, and when they had come, to

23

show them the object to be used to make connection with the subject of the investigation. After that the spirits would learn in some mysterious way where the subject was to be found, make the examination, and then, pass it on psychically to the reader. This procedure is universally denied by psychometrists. The same explanation is made of the mechanics of telepathy, and is even more unsatisfactory.

The second and more popular theory is based on the idea that the object handed to a reader to be "psychometrized", has been impregnated with the "radiations" peculiar to the subject. These radiations are said to create a "pattern" identical to that surrounding the subject. They must share the ability of the fabled "akasha" of India to record every event in the life of the subject as well as his appearance and characteristics.

If one can accept these complications, there remains the difficulty of proving that there is a force which can radiate in this patterned manner, and that it impregnates each and every object handled by the subject. Furthermore, there is the known fact that all radiant energy weakens rapidly as it spreads in all directions from the radiating source. This fact makes the radiation theory apply very poorly to such things as telepathy, for telepathic messages come in as strongly from across a continent as from across a room.

The Huna theory of the invisible ectoplasmic thread is much simpler. It replaces the complicated radiation theory and even explains how the spirits can follow established threads to make contact with either living or dead people.

The sticky shadowy body of the low self sticks

24

the end of a thread to everything touched, seen or heard, and this may at any time be followed regardless of distance to find the original person or thing to which the thread was fastened.

Following such a thread is like following a scent. But if the scent theory is insufficient to explain known facts, the thread theory can take over. In the cases where cats and dogs have successfully traced and followed their beloved masters for over a thousand miles, the several weeks taken for the feat rules out the theory that a scent was followed. Scents fade too soon to serve such a purpose. But the shadowy ectoplasmic threads connecting pet and master are enduring. They furnish the animal a means of making contact as in Psychometry and of learning where (or at least in what direction) the master travels.

So much for the Huna theory. If more details of it are desired, earlier books on the ancient lore may be consulted.

Closely allied to the subject under discussion is the field of water and mineral dowsing. Here the war still goes on between those who hold to the theory of radiations and those who believe that spirits find the things sought by the dowser with his forked stick or his complicated modern instruments. The Huna theory has but recently arrived on the scene, but is being considered.

Whether or not water or mineral bodies under the earth throw up radiations which are sensed by the dowser, or whether his low self projects a "finger" of *aka* substance through the intervening earth to find the desired flow or lode, one thing remains on which there is general agreement.

This is the fact that even while the dowser remains quite unaware that his muscles are moving the dowsing instrument or pendulum, if the latter is being used, the muscles do move and the rod dips or lifts, the pendulum swings, and the location is made. On the other hand, there is far less agreement as to what part of the dowser's consciousness causes the water to be found and the muscles to move to give the report through the code and instrument.

When a green willow or peach twig, cut to a fork, is used by a water dowser, there sometimes seems to be a force built up quite apart from the action of the muscles in the arms of the dowser. The fork may pull downward so strongly that if the pull is resisted with a very firm grip, the bark on the forked ends of the twigs will be twisted off.

This bark-twisting effect cannot be explained by saying that it is caused by unconscious muscular action on the part of the dowser, but the Huna theory of the possibility of the accumulation of vital force or "mana" in the aka substance projected into the fork, will offer an excellent explanation. The same theory also explains how poltergeists, or "noisy ghosts", store vital force taken from the living in their ghostly or shadowy (aka) bodies and can then move objects. The aka substance, even when invisible, will hold much mana, and when so charged, become alive, to all practical purposes, and can be used by the low self consciousness much as a flesh and bone arm can be used.

Just where involuntary muscular movement ends and the accumulation of mana-in-aka-substance in pendulum or dowsing fork or rod begins, is difficult to ascertain. Apparently there is usually a mixture of both mechanisms when such tools or aids are used to help the low self tell the middle self what it has found and what it wishes to report about it.

The readers of "Secret Science at Work" and of the Huna Research Bulletins will recall the important work of Mr. Verne L. Cameron, of Elsinore, California, who is an expert water and oil dowser. At the time of the reports on his work, he had invented an instrument to replace the usual forked twig or the pendulum used by most dowsers. He called it the "Aurameter", and it amounted to a rigid pendulum which is pivoted at one end and which can swing only sidewise. Its movement is free from the gravity pull which actuates the ordinary pendulum, and its sensitivity is of a different sort. It is a fine tool in the hands of a dowser trained to use it.

Mr. Cameron also invented another instrument which consists of a small weight fastened to the end of a metal bar and held almost at a vertical or upright position by a fine spring. It is so carefully balanced that at the slightest downward pull, as of gravity or from a magnet passed below it, the balance will be disturbed and the ball will fall downward. This is also a rigid pendulum, but is pivoted to move up-and-down instead of from side to side in order to respond to the pull of gravity.

This instrument, the "Psychogravimeter", was, at first, believed by Mr. Cameron and his friends to measure an actual increase in gravity. When held over a flow of underground water the weighted rod fell. This appeared to be caused by the natural gravity being increased above water which was moving under the earth. But other tests indicated no such increase. It became evident that something other than gravity was involved in the action of the instrument when held in the hand of a dowser.

Mr. Cameron soon made an additional discovery which threw light on the mystery. He built before him a purely mental image of a cylinder three feet in diameter and four feet long, standing on end. He wished to see whether a thought form or image of this kind was sufficiently substantial to be able to exert an influence on either his Aurameter or his Psychogravimeter.

When the Aurameter was held in the hand and brought close to the imaginary cylinder, its pendulum swung back away from the mental form as if pushed away by some repelling force.

When the Psychogravimeter was held over the cylinder, nothing happened. Then Mr. Cameron tried adding to his mental picture the power to exert a gravitational pull. This done, he again brought the instrument slowly over the invisible cylinder. As he did so, down fell the weighted pendulum, just as if it had been held over running, underground water.

Tests were run to see whether or not additional weight could be added mentally to an object set on a delicate pair of scales. No result was obtained.

Turning to Huna for an explanation of the actions of the Cameron instruments, we must conclude that the low self of the dowser (or user of the instruments) learns to cause the reactions of the pendulum heads to indicate to the middle self what it can sense concerning the presence of water under the earth. Likewise, the low self is reporting the fact that (1) a mental picture of a cylinder has been made and placed in a certain position, or (2) that the imagined gravity has been added to the cylinder.

If the Huna explanation is correct, and it seems by far the most reasonable, the whole of the mystery is reduced to something simple and easy to understand. There are no radiations measured by the dowser as they come up from hidden water. There is no repelling force in the imagined cylinder (or in the "aura" of a human body) which pushes away the pendulum tip of the Aurameter. There is no actual gravity added to the cylinder to pull down the pendulum end of the Psychogravimeter. There is nothing there but the low self of the dowser or instrument user. It is examining the things to which its attention has been directed and reporting its findings to the middle self by moving the dowsing rod, if one is in use, or the pendulums of the instruments when they are employed.

It must be admitted, of course, that all things do vibrate and radiate at a rate peculiar to themselves, even if this radiation may have little or nothing to do with the part played by the low self in doing its part in activities involving its psychometric abilities.

Mr. Cameron has discovered a strange force which is gathered by metal cones from the atmosphere, apparently, and is then condensed into a long ray which is projected as a "beam" for long distances. The beams can be located and measured by the low self when the Aurameter is used, but what the nature of their energy may be is still to be determined.

Mr. Cameron may not live to see the day when he will be acclaimed one of the great pioneers in the field of psychodynamics, being too far ahead of his times, but eventually his research will be recognized on all sides.

One of his most startling demonstrations has already made a "first" in history. In San Diego, before a group of amateur investigators in 1956, he asked that mental images of simple objects be made by the group while he remained outside the room. Upon returning to the room he took his Aurameter in hand and began to feel about with it to find and test the shapes of the thought forms which had been made ready. He located quickly thought forms of such things as globes, cones, vases and cubes. He even identified a mixed thought form image in which one of the group had implanted a globe in a cube.

Even more interesting was the test made in

which the group employed the medium, Mark Probert, to summon the spirit of one of his dead friends and request him to be present in the room in his ghostly body while Mr. Cameron tried to locate him with his Aurameter. The spirit willingly took part in the experiment, speaking through the entranced medium, and soon announced that he had hidden himself.

Mr. Cameron began feeling here and there in the room with his Aurameter, and soon found a place at which the pendulum was repulsed on approach. He quickly outlined with the instrument the form of a human body lying on the floor beneath a large table. "Here you are,"' he said. Through the medium's lips the spirit replied, "Yes, you have found me."

As time passes and research continues, it is increasingly evident that the low self possesses and uses psychic abilities quite foreign to the middle self. Some naturally gifted people are able to get from the low self mental pictures of the people or places or times involved in the course of making a psychometric reading. The low self may reproduce all the sensory impressions so that the reader may actually feel cold, hear sounds, taste tastes and so on.

But the majority of people are less gifted and such impressions seem not to be given them by their low self. However, the pendulum used in making a reading with the Biometer serves as a medium of communication which can be used by the low self of an individual with very scant psychic gifts to pass on its findings to its middle self.

The "pendulum talk" is simple, once a code of meanings is agreed upon to fit the various pendulum motions. To increase the scope of the communica-

31

tion system, scales of measurement are used and readings on them indicated via the pendulum. The term, "conventions" is used to describe the code.

It may be mentioned, in passing, that now and then when a reader has natural mediumistic leanings, the resident low self may give way to a spirit while a reading is in progress. In such cases the spirit may or may not help give a proper reading. As a rule, a spirit will take over only when questions are being asked of the low self by the middle self, and when the uninvited participant takes over the arm and causes the pendulum to answer the questions as it sees fit. Such answers are seldom correct, and should be allowed to play no part in the making of P.A. readings.

Chapter 5

As the primary purpose of this book is to help those who may be interested to learn to make readings of the Biometric or Psychometric kind, and to analyse them, the instruction can begin at once.

Some will learn to make readings with ease and will make them accurately. Some will learn more slowly and show less accuracy. Some will be unable to learn. In other words, a certain native talent or ability is needed, as in putting to use any of the ESP mechanisms.

The best way to find out whether or not one can learn to make P.A. readings is to try, and here is the way to set about it.

First one will need a pendulum because it is by means of the pendulum that the low self can tell you, the middle self, what it finds when making an examination of someone.

A very fine and elaborate pendulum may be made or purchased when one has found that such an instrument can be used successfully. For the purpose of testing one's ability, almost anything suspended from a thread or fine chain can be pressed into service.

The weight of a pendulum should be about that of a silver half-dollar. If scales are available, the pendulum can be made to weigh about one-half ounce.

A quick way to make a test pendulum is to take tin or aluminum foil and cut it into ribbons about one inch in width. Then wrap the ribbons around a small

33

darning needle allowing the eye and the point ends to protrude a half inch on either side of the rolled foil. Make the wrappings form a cylinder large enough to give the pendulum about the weight of the prescribed half-dollar. Pass a thread through the eye of the needle and tie a knot four inches from the needle's point. This knot is to act as a guide and should be between the thumb and forefinger when holding the pendulum ready for action. The protruding needle point is good because it is easily watched to see exactly what shape a swing may be taking when practice begins.

A finger ring or cross or other trinket from the jewel or tool or button box can also be pressed into use for the time being, but it is well to keep as nearly as possible to the 4 inch over-all length and to the one-half ounce weight as these will be retained when the permanent pendulum is decided upon.

Now find a pencil and a blank sheet of paper. On the paper draw some straight lines about two inches long and a circle about two inches across. (Or use those of the illustration on page 41.)

Next, address your low self. It is your younger brother or sister and it will be right there taking a great interest in all you are thinking and doing. It is always very much interested in anything that is new or different and which promises fun and something for it to do.

Say, "All ready? O. K. Let's pick up the new pendulum and hold it over one of the straight lines. I'll leave it all to you to see if you can make the pendulum swing. I'll just watch. Now let's see what you can do." You are holding the end of the pendulum thread at the knot which was tied at about four inches from the needle point, using thumb and forefinger. The paper with the lines and circles, or the book with illustrations, should lie on the table before you, so that your elbow may be rested easily on the table top or held slightly clear of it. Try both ways to see which one works best for you. If, after about a full minute of waiting, the pendulum does not move, take over and say, "Look. Do it like this, all by yourself, after I show you how." Move your hand and cause the pendulum to swing in a straight line in any direction, or make it swing along the straight lines before you in turn, then change and swing in a circle, following the circle on paper, first in a clockwise direction, then in a counterclockwise direction.

After showing the low self what to do, hold the pendulum over a straight line again and let the low self take over the arm and hand while you sit doing nothing more than keeping the pendulum suspended. Do not try to move the pendulum or to keep from moving it. Be relaxed mentally and physically. You will be "letting George do it", "George", in this case being your low or subconscious self.

Most people will get quick results, as almost anyone can get the pendulum response, even if he finds later that his low self is not capable of making a good and complete P.A. reading.

With the pendulum game started, the low self is asked to make the pendulum swing so that it will follow the straight lines, one after the other, then the circle, going clockwise (with the imaginary hands of a clock) or counterclockwise, at request.

The low self, "George", is very, very clever. It learns rapidly when it is interested, but is like a child in losing interest quickly and wishing to play some other game. It is also an individualist and may have prejudices and set ideas of its own. In the long series of experiments carried on by the Huna Research Associates, it was discovered that often the low self will like one form of makeshift pendulum and work with it, but not with another. One woman found that her low self would work only with a small china elephant suspended by a thread fastened to a ring in its back.

Once the low self will make the pendulum work as requested, it is time to establish a fuller contact or understanding and to carry on limited conversations through the medium of the pendulum and a set of "conventions". The usual convention for "yes" is a straight up-and-down swing of the pendulum. For "no" a swing from side to side is used, and for "I do not know" or "I am doubtful", a diagonal swing. Try out this code with the low self, teaching it by having it trace the three lines as mentioned. Then, when the sign language has been learned, begin asking simple questions and waiting for the low self to give answers as it may see fit. The conversation should be about simple things which require little reasoning power on the part of the low self. (It reasons only deductively, one must remember.)

Above all, do not make the mistake of asking the low self to be a prophet and to predict what is to be. It usually is anxious to please and often will try to do so by guessing when it does not know. If allowed to make guesses, and if it finds that its guesses cause excited interest, it will play up and show off, learning bad habits with childish eagerness. Only the High Self can see into the future, and then only a short distance as a rule. Ask the low self what it likes or dislikes, and why. Ask whether it thinks this or that or the other thing may happen. Never treat the answer as more than a guess. Take time to give your own (middle self) guess or opinion to offset any undesirable opinion which the low self may have expressed by way of the pendulum talk. If the low self should, for example, say it dislikes Mr. Boke, call attention to some of that gentleman's better traits or deeds. Be tolerant yourself and teach your low self to be tolerant lest you fall into the trap of making badly colored and incorrect P.A. readings of those whom you may not like or whom your low self may feel to be undesirable in various ways. Cultivate the calm and judicial attitude that it is necessary to hold if a correct reading is to be made, even if the subject is the Devil himself.

Once you are on good speaking terms with your low self, ask it if it will see what it can do about going to examine people and telling you what it can find. The low self will have shared the reading of this text with you and probably will already have a fair idea of the part it must learn to play in Psychometric Analysis. However, it is well to go over the matter step by step with it, practicing each step enough to get it fairly well acquainted with it before going on to the next. There are three steps or parts to a reading, and these can be taken in rapid succession, once all three are learned.

Chapter 6
LEARNING TO MAKE P.A. READINGS — THE CLOCK FACE

The first step in making a **P.A.** reading is very simple and easy. This also applies to the second. Only the third step is difficult.

In addition to the temporary pendulum, a second training tool is needed. This is a clock face without hands, or a drawing of one. It is just another means by which the low self can indicate to the middle self what it can learn. It is part of the general "convention" or code of communication. You may wish to use it always, or may soon prefer to imagine a clock face under the pendulum as you make the readings. Formerly, it was thought that a plate of metal must be used and the pendulum made to swing over it in taking the first two steps of the reading, but now we know that a paper sheet will do as well. On the sheet, for convenience, we have a design resembling a clock face, this being 2 inches across. (See Pg. 51.)

In order to begin practice work, one needs a few signatures written in ink, fluid ink being better than the thicker kind in modern ball-point pens. Pencil is poor for this purpose. Preferably, the signatures should be of people you know, so that you can check your readings by what you already know of the subjects. However, the better you know a subject, the more care you must take to hold the judicial attitude and avoid influencing the low self and coloring its findings.

Photographs can be used, or good reproductions

of photographs in newspapers or magazines. If a direct contact with the subject is possible, place your free hand, palm down, over the tip of the right thumb of your subject. (Over the left thumb tip if he is left-handed.)

If a signature or picture of the subject is to be used, place it just above the clock face. Then hold your pendulum over the clock face and while looking steadily at signature or picture, wait for your low self to reach out and contact the actual subject, examine him, and begin to swing the pendulum to tell you what it finds via the prearranged code.

M. Bovis, and Dr. Brunler after him, observed a strange thing. The pendulum seemed to make its own code or form of swing to fit certain characteristics of people or objects subjected to examination. For instance, the first reaction noted on the part of the pendulum was a movement in a straight line, back and forth. This line might take any direction, as from 12 to 6 o'clock on a clock face, or from 2 to 8 o'clock. This is called the "will" pattern of the middle self. We use a clock face so that we can more easily set down on our record the direction of this first pendulum movement in terms of clock time. For example, we may write down, "Will pattern at 12:45." This will indicate a straight swing across the clock face, passing through the center of it and touching the hour of 6:45 on the lower half. For convenience sake we do not write down the lower figure, simply the upper one on the clock face.

Often the "will" pattern will be made of more than one swing following one direction. After the pendulum has swung several times in one direction it will pause and then swing in another. This is

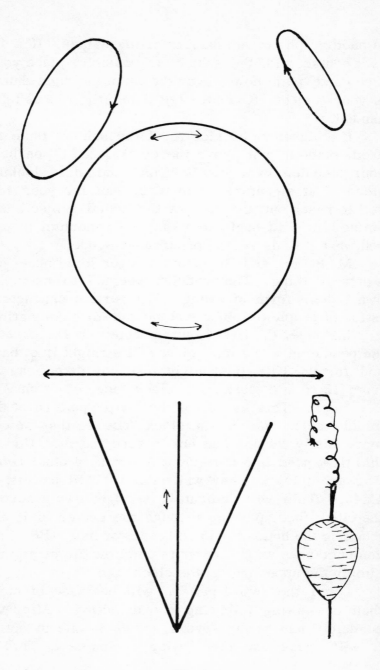

a "V" pattern, and one swing may be shorter and weaker than the other, the stronger side indicating the dominant "drive" of the middle self of the subject.

In the illustration it should be noted that 12:00 noon is the dividing point on the clock face between constructive drives and destructive. The swings to the right of noon are good. Those to the left are bad to some extent, even if the "V" pattern balances the drives for good and bad because this pattern indicates the subject is too easily influenced by others.

The "V" pattern in which the left side of the "V" is made by a very short swing, has been found to indicate the typical salesman who is not too careful in driving through a sale whether it is for the best interest of the customer or not.

The swing to the left of 12:00 noon is called a "counterclockwise leaning" swing, while a swing to the right of noon on the clock face is called a "clockwise leaning pattern". The vertical swing from the 12:00 noon mark down to 6:00 o'clock indicates the trained or perfected "will", and this is always part of the reading of an able hypnotist. To tell whether a hypnotist is good or bad, one must rely upon the second part of the reading in which the "personality circle" of the low self is described through the pendulum action. If the hypnotic "will" pattern happens to be accompanied by a counterclockwise "personality circle", the perfect will may be used for evil purposes.

Unfortunately, most of the people who show the "perfect" pattern appear to have achieved a powerful "will" control by much practice and, in the course of the practice, often have robbed the low self of its birthright to the degree that it gives almost no reading, or a very bad and destructive one.

41

The average "good" person who is blessed by a natural kindness and desire to be constructive will show a "will" pattern in which the straight swing is "clockwise leaning", that is, leaning in the clockwise direction away from the normal of 12 o'clock. A reading of 12:30 varying to one of 2:30 is desirable and it is usually an indication of a constructive drive and of tolerance.

The destructive and often criminally inclined usually have a "will" pattern in which the swing is counterclockwise leaning, or falling to the left of the 12 o'clock line. Any swing from 9 o'clock to 11:55 is to be looked upon as bad. If the second step reading of the low self "personality" gives a counterclockwise circle to go with the bad "will" reading, the subconscious needs watching. Dr. Brunler tested a large number of the inmates of prisons in England and found nearly all of them had a combination of the bad readings for both the low and middle selves.

In a very few readings there will be found three or even more "will" swings. In such cases the "will" of the subject may be unstable or there may be mental illness. Most frequently obsessional influences exerted periodically by the spirits of the dead are indicated. In obsession of this type, the victim may go berserk and commit deeds of violence.

In judging the meaning of the "will" pattern of a subject, it must be kept in mind that only the middle self is being described. As the low self plays an equally important part in the life of the man, it must be read and its nature and inclinations checked to see how they compare with similar items found in the middle self. Often a good middle self is teamed with a bad low self, and the good and constructive urges of one may be hampered by the destructive urges of the other.

While it is by no means certain just what it is in the middle self which we have come to call its "will" or "basic drive", the term "will" is used and the straight back-and-forth swing is used to indicate it, except, as noted, when the pendulum swings in a "V" pattern. We use this term for the "will" of the middle self to distinguish it from what is probably also "will" in the low self, but which we speak of as the "personality". The two readings can easily be told apart because that for the middle self is given only with straight swings, while that for the low self is given in circling swings.

As in all methods of measuring human traits or characteristics, we must have an arbitrary "norm" to use for the purpose of comparison. Our normal in reading the "will" pattern is a straight-line swing of the pendulum from 12 o'clock to six o'clock on or above the clock face. This is the "perfect" will, or, perhaps, the strongest. It is found, as has been said, most often in the readings made of practicing hypnotists. It is also found in readings of Hindu teachers of Yoga, Vedanta and similar systems.

If one is making a reading of a young child who is unable to write its name, its right thumb tip print, made with ink, may be used in place of a signature, or a photograph of the child may be used to allow the contact to be made by the low self.

Before one is ready to try to make a reading of the "will" pattern, which is the first step in making a complete reading, one must become familiar with the several meanings ascribed to the different swings of the pendulum or combinations of swings, as de-

43

scribed above. This is to make sure that the low self has learned at the same time that the middle self has learned, and so will understand just how to make the pendulum swing to tell what it finds when in contact with the subject.

The second step in making a reading follows at once after the low self finishes making the swings to tell what it has found out about the middle self "will" of the subject.

The pendulum is held in the same way over the clock face chart, and the low self will this time report in the code of circular swings what it has learned about the nature or "personality" of the low self of the one read.

The circular swing of the pendulum is clockwise if the low self has been found to be normally constructive and good. The circle described will be round instead of oblong. The size of the circle will be neither large nor small, but medium, and on the face of the chart such a circle has been made darker by having the hours and minutes indicated on it. It has also been given the letter "c" to indicate its size and to make it record the reading.

The circle reading is usually recorded by drawing a circle and placing an arrow head on the circumference to show that the swing was clockwise in direction. If the swing happens to be counterclockwise, of course, the arrow head will point in the opposite direction. The size of the circle will be indicated by the use of one of the letters placed on the chart to show the sizes of circles.

The size of a circle, whether clockwise or the reverse, will indicate the general health and vitality of the subject. One who is ill or weak or frail will often have a small circle of the "a" size. On the other hand, a very healthy and vital subject may have a circle of "e" size. In testing one's ability to accumulate a surcharge of vital force through deeper breathing and a command to the low self to take on a surcharge (as described in the book, "The Secret Science At Work"), a reading made after surcharging will show the circle perhaps increased to greater size than the outside circumference of the clock face.

The counterclockwise pendulum swing in making the circle indicates destructive drives on the part of the low self of the subject. If the "will" part of the reading is to the left of 12 o'clock, say at 11 o'clock, the destructiveness is shared by both the selves and so is much stronger, making for criminal tendencies very often. If the "will" swing is a "V", it will show the middle self to be half good and half bad, usually very easily influenced by others in either direction. Arch criminals with hypnotic "will" strength very often influence men of the "V" pattern type and cause them to join criminal gangs.

In deciding whether or not a criminal has been reformed and may be allowed parole without danger to the public, the Parole Board should have a reading made. If it shows that both selves are destructive, there has been no reform and no parole should be allowed. If the "V" pattern is noted and a counterclockwise low self or "personality" pattern circle is found, the criminal will be apt to slip back into his former ways unless he can be closely watched over by some determined good person after being paroled.

The pictures of criminals found in periodicals furnish excellent practice in learning to read for the destructive tendencies. The most brutal and vicious murderers frequently have readings indicating the destructive nature of the middle and low selves, and, in addition, show strong indications of either a type of insanity marked by fixations and delusions, or the periodic obsession by evil spirits.

The low self circle, oddly enough, seems to offer no clue to show whether the cause of the evil doing is based on fixations, delusions, compulsions or spirit obsession. It is possible that all these abnormalities of the low self are in some degree based on the influence exerted over the individual by evil spirits.

These departures from normal are shown by a flattening of the circle. Worries and uncertainty may flatten the circle slightly and only temporarily. The more dangerous condition is indicated by the fact that the circle is counterclockwise, and the narrowing down from circle to ellipse or to a shape resembling that of a double convex lens. The circle may thin down so greatly that it is almost a straight line like the "will" pattern swing.

If the thin and enlongated counterclockwise circle has an imaginary line drawn through it in its longest direction, this axis will remain unchanged if there is but one major fixation or one obsessing spirit. But if the pendulum keeps outlining the flattened circle in such a way that the axis changes, as from 10 to 11 of 12 o'clock on the chart face, more than one fixation or evil spirit may be suspected.

In making a reading of a medium, or in testing for mediumistic qualities, if the circle is clockwise, but tends to narrow and show a changing axis, the indication is that good spirits at times take over the body and use the voice of the entranced owner to converse with the living and give "messages". When a medium is read during a trance state—with a spirit in possession of the body—the reading will be of the spirit, not of the medium, and will show a decided difference when compared to the medium's reading taken while not in trance. In this way the goodness or badness of the communicating spirit may be learned. Some will be found good, and some bad, even if the latter make a great pretense of goodness.

The majority of the signatures which were obtained from inmates of mental hospitals for testing, showed counterclockwise-leaning "will" patterns as well as counterclockwise circles, greatly narrowed and with axes shifting from one position to another. Obsession is probable in most cases where the illness cannot be traced to physical causes.

Obsession seems usually to show in the "personality" circle, indicating (according to the Huna beliefs), that the spirits who are shown to be troubling the living are low self entities separated at death from their companion middle selves. Where both the "will" swings and the "personality" circles show signs of obsession, one may conclude that a spirit composed of the regulation two selves is involved.

In a very few readings it has been observed that only the"will" pattern changes in the direction of its swing several times. This, it has been concluded, may indicate obsession by a middle self entity which has been separated from its low self companion. In such cases the circle does not show a change of axis even though it may be much flattened.

The obsessing spirits of the normal or two-self type, if not bad, may be the cause of dual or multiple personality afflictions. If readings could be taken

48

at such times as different "personalities" were dominant or in control of those so afflicted, it is to be expected that a different reading would be provided by each spirit.

A very common cause of mysterious inner conflict and of a strange tendency to change from one mood to another, is the teaming up in one person of a clockwise and a counterclockwise pair of selves. It often is the middle self who has the constructive and good "will" pattern, while the low self shows in its counterclockwise circle that it is destructive and bad. The war between the good and bad selves will cause the person to be a frank and delightful friend part of the time, but secretive and vindictive at other times. Bright moods alternate with dark moods of anger and of unreasoning efforts to hurt others.

Now and then when a reading is made, either the "will" swing or the "personality" circle will fail to register. While the person being read may appear to be normal and healthy mentally and physically, it is a danger sign. Something is wrong and watchfulness is needed on the part of the one read and his close friends and associates.

This covers the first two steps of making a P.A. reading. So far, all is simple, and a majority of those who try to learn the art should succeed with ease up to this point.

In making the third step of the reading many will fall by the wayside. However, if one fails to be able to measure with accuracy the "degree" standing of those read, the standard I.Q. test results may be substituted for subjects above early school age.

Just to be able to make the tests of the first two steps will be a fine accomplishment and will help in endless ways in dealing with others, be they one's children, friends or complete strangers. The ability to separate the sheep from the goats in contacts with the business world is a great protection.

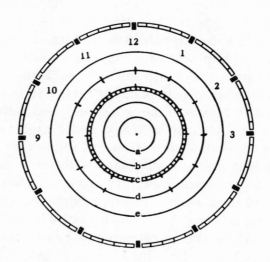

Above is reproduced the modified clock face now used in making readings by Psychometric Analysis.

Notice that the size of the circles is indicated by letters.

The straight swings of the pendulum above the clock face are indicated by setting down on the record the point in terms of time at which the swing has crossed the upper and outer edge of the clock face.

Later on we will have readings illustrated with lines drawn on the clock face to show where the pendulum swung.

The third step in making the P.A. reading is that of determining the over-all intelligence of the one being read.

The word "intelligence" is hardly adequate for this use for several reasons, mainly because it must include the form of intelligence peculiar to the low self, and at the same time the quite different reasoning intelligence of the middle self. One self may be a far more powerful member of the team than the other, and so throw the measurement off balance.

Dr. Brunler came to prefer to say that this third reading in terms of "degrees Biometric" gave the "sum total" measure of the "soul". He considered "soul" a poor description of the thing that makes up the whole of a unit of human consciousness, but explained that in English we have nothing better to use, our vocabulary being built around the concept of man as a one-self being. (Huna considers him a three-self being.)

"Intelligence" has two larger parts. These are memory and ability to reason. The low self does all the remembering for the individual and the middle self all the inductive reasoning. If the memory is especially good, a person with very poor reasoning ability can pass for one of high intelligence. On the other hand, a person with a poor memory but very superior reasoning ability may appear to be very dull while actually being very superior in intellect.

Despite the lack of differentiation between the elements of intelligence furnished by the two selves of the individual being read, the general reading in terms of "degrees" gives a better evaluation of the "intelligence" of the subject than does the modern "intelligence quotient". In the latter there is a similar failure to distinguish between the forms of mentation of the two lesser selves. Also the problem of age and experience must be considered in arriving at the final assessment of mental growth or evolution.

In the last analysis, as explained by Dr. Brunler, we are faced with the problem of measuring the evolutionary stage of growth or development of each one whom we attempt to read. This demands that we accept the theory of reincarnation as valid and look at soul evolution or growth as something connected with experience gained in a number of lives. Huna agrees with this point of view.

There has been much controversy over the exact reason why a pendulum held over various things should swing in such a way as to describe patterns in the air above them. Dr. Brunler thought the vibrations from objects caused the subconscious of the operator to make the pendulum move in a certain way. Over money or even a check drawn on a bank, his pendulum would always describe a "V" pattern. Over holy water the pattern was always a typical cross, and over the left hand a counterclockwise circle if the palm was up, and the reverse if the back of the hand were presented. In the instructions given in books on the use of the pendulum, authors state with confidence that over certain things, certain patterns will be marked out. However, it has been found that if a person is given a pendulum and asked to test the way it swings over the objects named, the prescribed motions usually will not occur unless the one who holds the pendulum is first made acquainted with the texts and has in mind what to expect. Other tests are equally potent in discrediting the theory that the object tested dictates the movement of the pendulum by the vibrations which it throws off.

What then must we decide? Simply that the low self of the operator picks up the vibrations or makes a sensory or psychic examination of an object or of a person, and then reports, through the pattern it marks out with pendulum swings the nature of its findings. If no established code or "convention" has been taught the low self so that certain swings can mean certain characteristics, it has no way of communicating to the middle self what it finds. And so, a "convention" we must have. Thanks to the pioneer work of Bovis and the later work of Dr. Brunler, we have in P.A. the agreed-upon code in hand. We can teach it to the low self, and it can then be used to report the findings of the low self when examinations are made. (See Chapter 10 for the degree code.)

The "convention" for the general or combined levels of intelligence is the "degree Biometric". It is a measurement of length, a degree being approximately 2 millimeters long or 100 degrees Biometric equaling about 8 inches.

While it seems absurd to say that we are able to measure intelligence in terms of distance, that is just what the "convention" suggests. Moreover, it is a workable method, just as is the determination of an "I.Q." in terms of numbers, with "normal" given an arbitrary value of 100, based on comparisons with set standards of intelligence rather than on any measure of the speed of vibrations or the distance between two objects.

In the case of the P.A. measurement of the intelligence, the Biometer appeared actually to be giving a reading based on real wave lengths or the distance between the tip of the subject's thumb and the edge of the metal plate over which the operator's pendulum was allowed to swing. As already related, Bovis went so far as to declare that the radiations or vibrations which were thrown off by tested objects were definitely related to radiations given off by the sun. Moreover, he said, the speed of light waves was exactly that of the emanations coming from the human body or other physical things.

Other workers with the Biometer have likened the radiations to vibrations on the string of a musical instrument, with points along the string at which it ceases to vibrate and a "chord" formation is noted. But, to make an end of confusing explanations, all can be swiftly simplified by saying that the "degree Biometric" is simply a convenient "convention" which is used to enable the low self to convey to the middle self through the pendulum its estimate of the overall intelligence of the person being examined.

This brings us to the practical side of the matter of learning to make a P.A. reading of the intelligence.

In order to establish in the mind of the low self a scale of values to use in reporting as a "convention", linear measure is used, in this case the degree Biometric.

One reads and impresses upon the low self the fact that intelligence is to be reported in terms of an arbitrary set of lengths. Bovis gave 100 degrees Biometric as the convention for perfect health and anything less than that indicated to him a health defect.

Dr. Brunler was responsible for setting the scale of measure to be used in measuring intelligence. He started the range of "brain radiations" at about 218 degrees Biometric for the mentally retarded, went on to 250 degrees for the average, and extended the scale to a theoretical 1000 degrees at which highest level the perfection of intellectual development might be found.

The highest actual reading he ever made, however, was 725 degrees, so the practical range of the Biometer became set at from 218 to 725 degrees for standard use. It remains the scale employed today in P.A. readings, and is sufficiently practical and adequate for most purposes.

Three things are needed to begin teaching the low self the meaning and use of the "convention" of the degree Biometric. These are a pendulum, one of the clock face paper charts or a substitute which measures 2 inches in diameter, and a temporary paper tape marked off in degrees Biometric and about 72 inches long.

You will already have supplied yourself with a pendulum, and the regulation clock face chart is to be found on the work sheets at the back of this book. Cut out a clock face and paste it on a paper so that you will have space for recording data; or you may trace the clock face on a sheet of paper.

On two sheets at the back of this book are reproductions of the Bovis measuring scale, with each of the sections 50 degrees Biometric in length. Cut these sections apart carefully and glue them end to end so that you will then have a complete paper tape which

55

will allow you to measure 900 degrees. Mark off the tape along its length to indicate 100, 200, 300, 400, 500, 600, 700, 800 and 900 degrees, using a colored or black wax pencil or lead pencil, but under no circumstance use pen and ink, as ink will hold your own shadowy thread and perhaps cause you to read yourself instead of the person whose inked signature you will be standing on the tape when making readings. Your tape can be mounted on a long strip of strong gummed paper, or upon a long narrow piece of wood if desired.

Once the tape is ready, lay it out on a large table and at the zero end place one of the reproductions of the standard clock face chart. The tape should extend to the left of the chart for right-handed people, but to the right of the chart for the left-handed. The pendulum is to be held over the chart with the right or left hand, whichever the operator finds best. The free hand will be used to move a signature or photograph progressively along the tape until the low self shows by the agreed-upon movement of the pendulum (held over the chart), that the proper degree on the tape has been reached.

Instead of a signature or photograph, one may make the reading directly from a subject, in which case the tip of his right thumb (left thumb for left-handed subjects) is placed at about the 240 degree mark on the tape and is very slowly moved along the tape away from the clock face chart until the action of the pendulum shows that the right degree on the tape for the reading has been reached. Signatures and pictures should have the paper below them folded so that they can stand alone, facing the pendulum, because it may be inconvenient to hold them all with your free hand while giving close attention to the swings of the pendulum. Moreover, if the subject is one blessed with a very high degree reading, the high point on the tape may be too far to reach without leaning far to the left and interrupting the pendulum swing for a moment. A helper to move the signature for you is a convenience, but be sure to tell your low self to read the signature and not the one moving it along the tape. The low self discriminates easily in such matters. A slot in a small block of wood to hold the signature or picture upright is convenient. The block may be slid along the tape and will stand at any point. In reading, allow for the thickness of the wood between the signature or photograph and the edge of the block. The reading must be the exact distance from the face of the signature to the zero mark on the tape.

If a metal plate is used instead of the clock face or if one draws a substitute circle, keep to the exact 2 inch diameter, otherwise the zero point on the tape will be moved nearer or farther from the center of the pendulum swing and will cause a variation in the degree reading.

The low self has a fine talent for measuring things, be they units of time, length, weight, temperature or variations in brightness, color, softness or hardness, and so forth. It is a great hand at counting things and comparing them. For this reason the use of a scale of linear measure is excellent for our purpose.

Once the low self grasps the idea that it is to indicate to the middle self through the use of the pendulum, and in terms of "degrees" of a given length, what it can learn in making a reading of a person for intelligence, the work can proceed almost at once. A little practice will probably be all that is necessary providing the reader has sufficient natural talent to bring to the work.

Steps one and two must be mastered before beginning the work of teaching the low self to make the degree reading. But when ready to begin work on the degree step, one proceeds as follows:

With the tape anchored on a board or table with the zero mark touching the left edge of the printed rim of the clock face, a signature or picture is made to stand upright on the tape at the 240 degree point. This point is to be used because only those of undeveloped mentality will show readings below that.

Now hold the pendulum (which should be 4 inches from tip to knot in thread where it is held) over the center of the clock face chart. Turn your eyes to look at the signature or picture and wait for your low self to make contact and give you the "will" pattern reading. Either pause to record it or remember it and go ahead to get the "personality" circle. Record or remember it for later recording, and then try for the degree reading. (It is well to get into the habit of starting each time with the first step and going right through all three one after the other).

The low self will have been taking in what you have been reading about the measurement of the intelligence of the subject in terms of the distance between the edge of the chart and the signature or picture, this distance to be expressed in terms of the degrees Biometric. If in doubt whether or not the information has been absorbed, try to remember the details of the explanations which have been given. If the low self, who does all the remembering for its

man, can recall the details, be sure that it has miss-
ed nothing. Go ahead with confidence to let it try
its hand at measuring the intelligence of the subject
and telling you, via the pendulum, what it is.

The convention or code at this point is very easy
to understand. When the signature is moved to the
left along the tape, slowly, while the pendulum continues to swing in a straight line, the correct place
on the tape will be signalled by the low self by making the pendulum swing exactly up and down over the
12 o'clock point of the chart. When the signature has
not been moved far enough, the swing will be off to
the right of 12 o'clock, usually over 1:30 o'clock. If
the signature has been moved too far along the tape,
the swing will cross over the 12 o'clock point and begin to swing to the left of it, perhaps over 10:30.

The low self will soon get the knack of using the
code and will quickly tell you just where to stop the
signature on the tape and read the degree number
just under its front edge. If it chances to be 350,
record this as the degree reading. If uncertain as
to the correctness of the reading, politely ask your
low self to repeat. If it is tired, rest a minute or
two and then start all over, going right through all of
the three steps.

Reading is hard and tiring work for the low self.
Even when one has become expert in the art, it is not
good to make more than five readings at a sitting,
and a few minutes at least should elapse between the
readings. If the low self is allowed to become too
tired, it may come to dislike the work and refuse to
take part in it. Or, it may try to make things easy
for itself by reading all subjects with the same result
in each case as if it were reading its own man. Take

things slowly, especially during the training period.

Incidentally, making a reading for oneself is not too sure or too satisfactory. One may try it, using signature or picture, but the chances are that the low self will either have a wrong opinion of itself and its middle self or of their combined intelligence. An inferiority complex will cause the reading to be far too low, while a "delusion of grandeur" may cause the degree to be too high to register on the scale.

When one has learned to make degree readings well with the use of the tape, it is time to begin to teach the low self to give the reading without using the tape.

The tape is a convention, nothing more. No actual radiating waves take off from the zero point to impinge on the edge of the chart and register their length. The "degrees Biometric" are strictly an arbitrary measure of intelligence. The convention could just as well have been constructed in terms of pints and quarts, or of degrees of heat or cold. We are working with pure psychometry, not with any known form of radiation. The very fact that we can throw away the tape and continue to use the convention which it represents is proof that waves are not being measured.

The low self can estimate distance or the time of day with much accuracy. With the mental picture of the tape it needs nothing more. Once the middle self has seen this point, the practice can begin. The tape is set aside and the pendulum held directly over the chart above which has been laid the signature or the picture from which the reading is to be taken.

For readings where the exactness of the pendulum swings or circles is not demanded, the pendulum can be held directly over the thumb tip of the person to be read. Imagine the clock face chart as lying between the thumb tip and the pendulum if desired, and go on with the reading. When the "will" and "personality" readings are finished, picture in mind the tape and imagine that you are starting the degree test at 240. Silently instruct your low self to count 10 degrees to each complete back-and-forth swing of the pendulum while you count silently by tens to keep track of what the pendulum is ticking off.

Counting by ten degrees at a swing enables one to go faster. One degree to a swing could, of course, be used, but it would take longer than necessary.

An example will explain the next point. Say that a reading is to be made of a person with a standing of 318 degrees. One starts, as already instructed, with "240", and as the pendulum continues to swing, the count keeps pace with, "250, 260, 270, 280, 290, 300, 310, 320." With the count of 320 the actual or correct degree reading of 318 has been passed and the low self will learn to stop the swing abruptly, often jerking the wrist of the hand which holds the pendulum. Once the swing has stopped, one goes back ten degrees, in this case to 310 degrees, and starts anew, but now counting by ones, as, "310, 311, 312, 313, 314, 315, 316, 317, 318," at which point the low self again stops the pendulum from swinging.

Once one has learned, or perhaps we should say, once the low self has learned, to work without the tape, readings can be made much more rapidly and easily. However, the tape should be saved for a time in case there arises a doubt as to the accuracy of the purely psychometric method and one wishes to run a check, using the tape, just to make certain that the low self is working carefully. A few readers may not be able to graduate from the use of the tape, but most can with a little practice.

It is even possible for some good readers to get to the point where it is possible to imagine even the pendulum, and to watch it with an inner sense while it ticks off a degree reading of someone across the room or even of an actor appearing on the television screen. Dr. Brunler often tried to tell at a glance what a reading would be, and was always much pleased when a later test on the Biometer proved his snap-reading to be correct.

Chapter 9
Evaluating the Information

Once the reading with its three parts or stages is completed and written down, work of evaluating the information furnished by the low self through the pendulum and the "code" must be undertaken.

Thanks to Dr. Brunler, the general outline of the meanings has been worked out. This gives sufficient guidance for present uses, but it may take years still before the finer points are properly understood.

Under the Brunler system and theory, the man was handled as a conscious mind being with a subconscious part. This fits the Huna idea of a middle and low self.

In the light of the ancient Huna beliefs, it became evident that the "will" and "personality" readings best fitted the middle and low selves, respectively. The chief argument in favor of this conclusion is that the obsessions, complexes and hidden anxieties indicated in the "personality" circle reading are almost always quite unknown or unrecognized by the one being read.

The conclusion that the High Self is implicated in some way in part of the "degree" reading came from a series of experiments carried out soon after the Brunler system was taken on by the Huna Research Associates for investigation and study. In the course of tests a large number of readings were first made of participating HRA members. Then the same members tried writing down their signatures in ink just after careful efforts had been made with the Huna-type prayer and meditation to contact the High Self, to see if they had been able to raise their "degree" or "vibration" standing. These signatures were read and compared with signatures written without efforts to contact the High Self, the result being that in over half of the tests the rise was at least 50 degrees, and in a few cases the rise was over 100 degrees.

In these experiments the "will" and "personality" patterns also showed marked changes. Usually the "will" swing was much weaker and more clockwise-leaning, a swing read at 1:05 on the chart becoming 2:15 or even dropping almost to 3:00, which indicated almost no action of "will" at all on the part of the middle self. Apparently there was complete submission to the High Self will. The "personality" circle reading of the low self usually increased in size and strength. If it had been off-round normally, it rounded out for the time being, returning to the imperfect smaller circle in a short time.

Still another peculiarity was noted and studied. This was that when a surplus of vital force or "mana" had been accumulated, the low self circle increased often to double its size while retaining its rounded or distorted normal shape. But when contact with the High Self was made and the vital force was sent to it by the low self (on command of the middle self, and along the connecting invisible or "aka" cord) the circle diminished in size to almost nothing, even while holding, temporarily, the typical perfect roundness. In passing, it is interesting to note that no HRA with a counterclockwise circle swing participated in the tests.

Dr. Brunler observed these tests with much interest and speculated that when a man evolves to the limit of perfection, he should stand at the High Self or "Master" level. In an effort to gain added information on this point he ran Biometer tests on a photograph of the famous "Shroud of Turin", this being, he believed, a cloth which had covered the face of the dead Jesus, the contact leaving the imprint of his face upon it.

Dr. Brunler's reading was 1,000 degrees Biometric, and he took this to be the ultimate of soul growth or evolutionary progression Godward. The point was brought up at once that the "Shroud" might be, like so many other "holy relics", spurious. It was well known that the opinions of the reader will all too often influence his readings, therefore more tests on such photographs were in order. As might be expected, those of the HRA who ran check readings got no degree indication at all when they were of the opinion that the Shroud was spurious. On the other hand, two who believed in the genuineness of it got the same reading as had Dr. Brunler, each, of course, knowing what he had reported as his degree reading. Later on, photographs were collected of several of the most famous "holy men" of India. It was hoped that some of these had reached the high state of "masterhood" (using the Theosophical meaning of the term). But a surprising thing developed. These teachers and leaders of India, many deep in Yoga lore, invariably showed the perfect "will" of the type we had come to associate with hypnotists, and also the well rounded, large and clockwise circle of the low self "personality" pattern. Only one gave a degree reading above the 365 level, and in one

65

case there was a counterclockwise circle reading. This threw doubt on the gentleman's qualification for inclusion in such illustrious circles. The only conclusion of value which was reached was that men who perfect their "will" and bring the low self into a full state of perfect normalcy, as indicated by a well rounded "personality" circle, need not have evolved out of the 340 to 365 level to become great teachers, at least teachers of things in which they have come to believe.

Dr. Brunler, in testing a girl of such weak intellect that she had barely been able to learn to tell her right hand from her left when asked, decided that her reading, 218 degrees, marked only a few degrees above the lowest or beginning level of human intelligence. In the HRA it was decided, much later, that this might be the beginning of the level at which the low self joined to function as part of the man (leaving the High Self out of the calculation for the moment.)

Dr. Brunler speculated that the level between 100 and 200 degrees might belong to the subconscious alone, but his ideas on this subject seem never to have crystallized into a permanent opinion.

In the HRA a study was made to try to throw a little light on the matter. Unfortunately, the Huna lore contains little or nothing to suggest that the man has not evolved from the bottom upward. The low self evolves from the animal selves, and later, the same self evolves into a middle self and lives with a low self for that stage of its progress, eventually blending with a self of the opposite sex and graduating into a male-female High Self, at which time it assumes the task of helping and guiding a low-middle self pair.

The only alternative to this idea of evolution is to be found in a theory which is at least as old as Egypt. It is that when animals evolved to the point at which the human animal was capable of accepting the guidance of a higher form of intelligent being, the "gods" descended and took up residence in the body of the animal man, furnishing the element of inductive reason and a superior form of "will" power to make man as we know him. In this theory of the evolution from the top down to meet the upward growing animal self, the place of the High Self as a form of "guardian angel" self is left unfilled.

The problem is left very much up in the air no matter which point of view is favored. One wonders how basic evolution could begin with the simplest of microscopic life forms and evolve upward through the complications of man and human consciousness unless there existed from the beginning a fully evolved and perfected Conscious Something to make the blueprints of creation, then stand by to supervise every step of the building. The materialistic suggestion of Science that this Higher Intelligence is contained in the substance and life forms shaped from it, is difficult to accept.

As we do not have to solve this greatest problem of religion and science, we can proceed happily to work on the lower levels with what knowledge we now have. We can be sure that the growth is upward toward a continual broadening and expanding of the field and scope of consciousness.

Chapter 10

SUMMARY OF DR. BRUNLER'S FINDINGS

By a study of thousands of readings, Dr. Brunler was able to generalize when describing the meaning of the degree levels, Biometrically speaking.

The 240 to 300 level appeared to contain those who work with the hands rather than with the heads. The average intelligence in backward lands was said to be 240 degrees. In Europe and the United States, 250 degrees. At 240 the worker must be told just what to do at every step of the way, but if taught, can learn simple things like digging, carrying and so on. At 250 the intelligence increases and less guidance is needed. By 260 the skill of the hands becomes much better, increasing with each degree. At 275 the intelligence is greater and the worker begins to be able to act as foreman and to oversee and teach others.

At 282 the ability to sell "tangibles", such as cars and houses, is marked. At 288 to 300 are found the top foremen and most skilled hands. Here there is much "horse sense" and ability to work out ways of doing things. But in this level the mind clings to the material world and fails to grasp the abstract. Here the abstract concept of an intangible God is rejected. God must be thought of as "in the likeness of man" or not at all. Here are the fanatics of the orthodox churches. Once they accept a certain set of beliefs, their minds seem to close to all arguments against those beliefs. Men who think in the terms of the abstract are looked upon with suspicion and are call-

68

ed "egg heads". Any effort to influence or to "con-
vert" people of this level must be through an emotional appeal which acts on the low self, it being
the very child of the emotions. If the emotional appeal carries with it the urge to fight in defense of
something or for something yet to be gained, the result will be even more marked. The emotional ap-
peals of the revival meeting, the war drums and the
most clever modern advertising bear their best fruit
at this level. As 90% of mankind is found to be in
this level, it is thus that the world is swayed for good
or bad by the more intelligent few of the still higher
levels. (Higher levels contain as large a number of
evil people as do lower levels.)

At 300 degrees, Dr. Brunler found skill with the
hands growing less while the memory seemed to become especially good. From 300 to 318, languages
are easily learned, as is music "played by ear".
Here the student, because of the superior memory,
may appear far ahead of his fellows in school, but
often fails to grasp and solve problems in arithme-
tic, or to make a good showing in handicrafts. The
splendid penman of the level below vanishes, and in
this level one too often scrawls or is forced to print.
One sings, perhaps, but seldom plays an instrument
well. Memory replaces the safe lesser reasoning of
"good horse sense" and the thinking often becomes
warped and strange.

Efforts to adjust to surrounding conditions often
result in peculiar makeshifts, and too often a dangerous imitation of crafty cleverness develops. In
this level are found many criminals, and, as they
are not rational in their craftiness, they soon end in
a reformatory, jail or prison. If they have a low

self counterclockwise personality circle, coupled with a "will" pattern falling from 9:00 to 12:00 o'clock on the chart face, or if they have a "V" pattern falling first to the left of 12:00 and then to the right, they are prone to become criminals on their own initiative or through the influence of other criminals.

Those with the "V" patterns are easily influenced at any and all of the levels. Some of the most cold-blooded and conscienceless murderers of the century have had a degree reading of between 300 and 315.

From 318 to 320, there seems to come with the slight evolutionary growth a reaction which produces men and women of extraordinary natural goodness. Ministers, missionaries, teachers and "do-gooders" of all sorts are found here.

From 320 to 330 the low self is showing growth. It keeps its excellent memory, but because there is still a lack of reasoning power to replace the "horse sense" of the lower levels, a strange ability begins to develop. It is the ability to read minds, and if there is someone present who knows a desired answer to a problem the person in this level often can read the other's mind and get the answer. At this level the excellent memory may allow the individual to take a college education, but the lack of superior reasoning power may make it impossible to use the education in a way to make a living in any other profession than that of teaching or politics.

The level from 330 to 355 sees the psychic powers continuing to grow and the reasoning powers increase steadily so that medicine and law can be practiced with some success. The doctor may unconsciously use his psychic powers to help in his diagnosis of a patient's ills, but, all too often, he will

70

read the mind of the patient and accept that reading as a correct indication of what is causing the illness. At 350 degrees the peak is reached for the user of the lesser level of psychic powers—the lower intuition as in contrast with the higher intuition that begins to show above 450 and is at its best at 550.

Dr. Brunler visited and read fortunetellers and spirit mediums all over London, finding them all very close to the 340 to 350 level. The fortunes they told were simply reading the hopes and fears in the minds of patrons and feeding these back to them as things apt to happen in the future. Mediums in the same level appeared to allow spirits with mindreading ability to take control of them, and these also fed back the hopes and fears as things about to happen. Real ability to see into the future was so rare as to be, for all practical purposes, missing.

Another form of psychic ability which begins at 350 degrees and which extends to show again with increased excellence at the 450 and 550 degree range, is that of the water and mineral "dowser". Here we also find the best hands at the use of the Biometric or Psycho-Analytical methods. Dr. Brunler made readings at a conference of dowsers and found that in doing map dowsing for water (locating water at points on a map set before them, even when the mapped territory might be a thousand miles distant) the contact which was made and held psychically with the land shown on a map could be held for only a minute by dowsers of the 350 degree reading. But, as the degree readings rose, the time increased. One of the dowsers tested had a reading of around 550 degrees, and he could hold contact for a full five minutes. These men used pendulums or dowsing rods over the maps just as if over the actual ground when working to find water in the field. Oil and minerals are more difficult to locate by map dowsing, gold being the most difficult of all.

According to the Huna explanation, the clever low self of the dowser will extend a shadowy "finger" of its ectoplasmic body to find the place indicated to the middle self by the map. Once in such contact, it can explore the depths of the earth, locate the desired substance, and indicate its presence on the map by causing the rod to dip or the pendulum to swing in the agreed-upon way. All other theories proposed to explain map dowsing depend on sensing radiations, but it is difficult to accept the radiation theory when a great distance is involved between the dowser and the mapped plot. Another explanation is that the spirits of the dead, nature spirits, angels or even the High Selves assist in map dowsing.

The level from 360 to 370 degrees finds changed psychic abilities. Mediumistic and mind reading abilities fade, but the ability to use the pendulum or dowsing rod increases greatly. Here is also found a marked ability to use Psychometric Analysis such as we are discussing, or to use the "radionics" instruments invented in the past few decades for diagnosis and treatment of disease as well as other experimental purposes. On most of these machines neither the pendulum nor the dowsing rods are used, but instead, the fingers are rubbed on a smooth block of material, the "code" being that the fingers seem to be sticking to the rubbed block, this indicating the point at which the reading is to be taken from the dials of the instrument. As the turning of the dials can do nothing more than change slightly the distance over which an electrical current could pass, if there were an electrical current used (which there is not), one must conclude that the psychic element of the operator is what really controls the reactions or actions supposedly resident in the instruments themselves. Photographic films have been placed in such instruments, and with the right operator, apparently pictures of distant objects have been taken, even of events occurring in the past, as with the De la Warr instruments now being studied by a group in England.

This level produces the best physicians and dentists. They have a certain psychic ability to help them diagnose the cause of ills, and possess, as a rule, a fine mechanical ability coupled with natural skill in the use of the hands. Here are found most of the clever surgeons. Skilled commercial artists are at their best here, but artists painting in oils seldom rise above the mediocre. Teachers thrive on this level except for those professors of the university posts who usually come from the next level. The talents of this level are many and varied. The thinking ability and range of interest is marked. Being able to do so many things well, the native of this level may have to avoid a tendency to be a "jack of all trades, and master of none." Salesmen in this level can sell insurance and other "intangibles". The will power of the middle self often needs strengthening in this level by exercises in concentration. Children of the level should be taught to stick with a project when once started. The tendency is to give up almost before making a good start. The world is opening up to them and too many fascinating new things keep coming into view to demand their attention.

The narrow level from 370 to 385 degrees finds

people in it who seem to be expanding their horizons so that they have a constant stream of new interests. They can do almost anything fairly well, but seldom wish to stay with one line of endeavor long enough to master its techniques. Here are the curious ones who are not satisfied with the accepted explanations which are offered to cover events in nature or beliefs in religion. They are never tired of searching for new facts, and when they have assembled those facts, they set about constructing a theory to fit them, often coming up with something more bizarre than useful.

In this level are found teachers, judges, reporters and people operating small businesses based on something novel. The "idea man" is at home here, but the level is not noted for its down-to-earth practicality. Again we have the good starters who are apt to be poor finishers.

The level between 385 and 400 degrees sees the horizons grown still wider, and again the memory may become outstanding. With a fine memory and fair reasoning ability, learning is rather easy and often tempting. Dr. Brunler called this the "Professor Range" because he found in it so many who had gravitated to chairs in great universities. He also found a general tendency to be orthodox and to accept the authority of the text book rather than bestir oneself to learn whether current scholastic dogmas were sound. If the professor writes, he seldom does more than examine the texts in the field and draw from them material for a text better suited to his tastes. Here is the book worm who likes to lecture and to teach, but who is disturbed if some student asks too penetrating questions or challenges the authority of the current texts.

The level between 400 and 410 degrees was called by Dr. Brunler, "The Fear Range". In it he had found men and women of exceptional mental ability who, all too frequently, were afraid to use it. Their ability to make a decision was poor and they were prone to give their best ideas to others and to let them present them as their own. This is the home of the brilliant person who continually surprises those about him by his impractical and roundabout efforts to accomplish such things as his scant confidence may allow.

At 410 degrees, and rising to around 450, come the leaders in business. They are blessed with wide vision, good reasoning power and fair memories. As to confidence, they have almost too much of it. If uneducated, they will become the big frog in whatever small puddle they find themselves. If well educated, they climb to the top, often over the bruised backs of those who may happen to be in the way. They head the great corporations, and the higher level of psychic ability which they possess often makes them appear able to outguess rivals in judging the future of business trends.

From 450 to 550 degrees genius becomes apparent. At 550 the writers whose works endure dot the pages of history. There the most famous of the generals stand out in history, perhaps for good, or perhaps for evil. The lesser painters belong here, and here the famous composers of music flourish.

The level from 550 to 725 degrees is that of the highest development of mind and intellect, but very few have attained it and left behind a signature on manuscripts or paintings so that their P.A. readings can be taken. Dr. Brunler searched museums and art galleries, often pressing a packet of table salt to a signature on a great painting or treasured document to let the salt absorb what he thought to be the radiation from the signature, then later took a reading with his Biometer from the salt. It made little difference whether or not the writer of the signature was dead or alive, the reading could be made.

Even higher than the famous composers stood the great painters. And, highest among these, the painter, sculptor, inventor and man of so many fine talents, Leonardo da Vinci. He stood at 725, highest of all.

Dr. Brunler, who read himself at over 700 degrees, gave the following readings in one of his Los Angeles lectures:

Thomas Edison, inventor, 470 degrees.

Mme. Curie, discoverer of radium, 492 degrees.

Emerson, famous essayist, 500 degrees.

Kipling, famous for short stories, 527 degrees.

Charles Dickens, lasting novels, 540 degrees.

Haydn, composer, 538 degrees.

Liszt, composer, 538 degrees.

Chopin, composer, 550 degrees.

Rembrandt, painter, 638 degrees.

Titian, painter, 660 degrees.

Tests of great actors and actresses showed that they come in the 450-550 degree level. Readings of actors who fall below this level show that they must depend on their lines and the impersonation of such characters as they portray. But in the high levels they can hold their audiences endlessly just from sheer artistry and personality.

When one has learned to make a P.A. reading, it is most enlightening to sit down to read from the illustrations of magazines showing the pictures of people in the news. The majority will be of lower degree levels, and as one goes up the scale, fewer and fewer will be found. Perhaps only one in a million has a reading above 500 degrees.

When election time comes around, the real value of candidates can quickly be assayed through readings, and the constructive can be told from the destructive through the "will" and "personality" patterns.

In contemplating business deals with those who may or may not be reliable, a reading taken from a signature or picture will be of great value. Selecting a doctor, a lawyer, a helper or even a mate, may be made easier and safer with the aid of the P.A. readings.

In working with children, a reading can be made from a thumb tip direct, or from an inked thumbprint showing the tip of the thumb. Readings change but little in the course of a lifetime unless conscious effort is made to correct and raise them. A growth of six degrees was considered by Dr. Brunler to be unusual.

The "will" pattern is the easiest to correct, and this can be done by training in concentration. The "personality" pattern changes if one retrains the low self when a faulty circle is found. Checks on progress in these endeavors can be made at any time through a fresh reading.

In evaluating the general reading, care must be taken to consider the influence of each part of it on the whole. For instance, a high degree reading in the third step may be accompanied by a "will" swing or pattern along the 11 o'clock tangent of the chart while the "personality" circle may be clockwise and of "c" size, but badly flattened and given an axis at 2:15 o'clock. The degree indicates a high level of intelligence if it is above 330. However, the counter-clockwise leaning "will" pattern indicates the tendency toward destructive or dishonest actions. But the low self reading shows a tendency to be constructive and basically good, even if the flattened circle indicates that the middle self has browbeaten and dominated it to a great extent. The combination points to a continual inner war, and perhaps a constant effort on the part of the individual to justify himself for the evil done. One would say, "Have a care in dealing with this person. Marry him at your peril."

Speaking of marriage, a P.A. reading can often show whether or not an individual is a suitable mate. People with similar degrees and patterns have the best chance for mutual understanding and neither of the marriage partners will have to make continual allowances for character defects or a lower level of intelligence. A pair matched in goodness will get on with ease while a pair, one of whom is destructive, will never see eye to eye.

A man of the 390 degree level who is married to a 350 woman may be constantly annoyed when she keeps saying that she knows this or that but can give no reason for her conclusions. He is logical and will want to know why she thinks or feels as she does. She is intuitive and a natural mind reader, or may be psychic and in touch with spirits who give her warning feelings about people or proposed actions. If such a couple can have readings made and each be brought to understand the mental approach natural to the other, they can then reach an understanding and make the proper allowances for their differences.

When it comes to protecting oneself or others, if a close association is to be made in any way with a person who has not been known and observed for several years, the most valuable test with P.A. is the one for variations in the pendulum action when a reading is made.

With a normal person the pendulum will swing in a steady way, and repeat on request the action which signifies the reading. But with the abnormal person who may have hidden defects in the "will" or the low self "personality", there is to be observed a change of the pendulum action as if the reading were being made for several persons at the same time. If the "will" swing keeps changing to different clock face readings and back to the original starting point, it is to be guessed that there is a defect in the middle self control of the mind. This may be caused by the influence of spirits who take over and control the person part of the time and who remain close, but not in control, the rest of the time. These hidden entities cannot be detected by ordinary observational means, but the reading shows them to be present.

The reading to get the "personality" circle may show variations in which the pendulum performs as if the reader could not make up his mind. The size and form of the circle may change slowly, giving two or more elements to be considered. Such variations often indicate fixations and compulsions, not infrequently complicated by the presence of spirits who act on the low self rather than on the middle self.

In marked insanity, both of the types of variation described above will be seen in the reading, growing more and more pronounced as the obsession becomes

79

complete and the patient loses control of both his selves to the obsessing spirits.

Modern doctors and psychologists generally refuse even to consider the possibility that the spirits of the dead can influence the living. Many names are used to describe the slight influence exerted by the spirits on the living, but when the spirits take over completely, the ancient term, "obsession", is still used.

To avoid the admission that there are spirits, the doctors are forced to propound the lame theory that the "self" of a man can be split into one or even several parts.

A "split personality" victim may have several "parts" which may take over or obsess the victim in turn. Some take over both the middle and low selves while others take over only one of the selves. But, and this is what makes the theory so hard to accept, the obsessing "parts" often show that they are as perfect as another person would be, having other sets of memories, other likes and dislikes, and quite different states of health or degrees of intelligence, these being noted in the victim as the spirits take possession.

Huna gives us a complete explanation of this and other phases of spirit activity in which the living are influenced slightly or greatly.

An important point to remember is that these spirit troubles often do not become apparent for a number of years in the lives of those naturally open to such invasions. Shocks, illness and mental strain may allow the unnoticed effects to become marked.

If the P.A. reading of a seemingly normal person shows the "will" swing changing slowly from side to side over the chart face, the indication is that the middle self is influenced in its drives and even in its thoughts by the outside influence. A regular "V" or single-slant reading is normal, but three directions of swing is not, except in the case of a hypnotist, who not infrequently will show a swing at 12 o'clock in addition to his native or normal swing pattern.

Most often the trouble is indicated by variations in the "personality" circle of the low self. Any variation should be looked upon as a danger sign. In the young, or in those who, upon examination, may show no signs of the influence of spirits or of reactions to fixations, trouble may become apparent later.

"Forewarned is forearmed," says the old saw. The things to be watched for are changes in moods or emotional life. A sudden compulsion accompanied by an unaccustomed set of emotions should not go unheeded at any time.

The victims of these outside influences involving spirits (but not fixations or complexes caused by emotional or physical shocks), according to Huna lore, can often protect themselves, once they know that such influences are around them, by steadfastly staying on the "good" side in every thought and deed. The spirits are said not to stay with those who refuse to respond to their subtle promptings and who refuse to be as basically evil as the spirits are. A fixation or complex may be uncovered and "drained off" by psychiatric methods, but as long as the reality of spirit obsession remains unrecognized by the psychiatrists and psychologists, only "shock" treatment remains to be used, this making it so uncomfortable for the spirits that they sometimes leave.

The value of the P.A. readings can hardly be overestimated. On the other hand we must remain fully aware of the fact that this is a measuring system based on the use of the psychic faculties, and therefore more than usually subject to errors.

To avoid errors in readings is of the greatest importance. Those who read this book should do all that is possible to find a few friends who will also try their hands at learning the use of the P.A. methods. Only when several people have worked long enough to become proficient readers, can results be compared and the general accuracy of the several readers of the group be determined.

Even the experienced reader often needs someone to run a check to be sure that any particular reading is correct. Despite the greatest care, the middle self may color the reading of the low self by holding to a preconceived idea of what the reading should be.

If a reader is given a signature or photograph of a stranger and is told that he is a college president, the expectation of a high level of intelligence may cause an error of many degrees. The less one knows of the person being read, the better for the accuracy.

In making a P.A. of an infant or child under five, the reader must take the greatest care, and a check, or even several checks, may be needed if anxious parents are present or are well known to the reader or readers. Any sympathetic person will, almost in spite of himself, be influenced by the hopes and desires of the parents to read the degree level too high or to cover up the defects which should show in the "will" and "personality" tests.

Readings made with the Biometer, where direct contact is made with the one being read, seem to be a few degrees higher on the average than similar readings made from the signature. This can only be accounted for by the natural wish on the part of the reader to be kind or complimentary to a subject who is present in person. To be sure, a direct reading should be followed by one made from a signature, and to be further sure, a check should be run by a fellow reader.

Of course, one should be very kind and considerate at every step. The reader is accepting a confidence and this involves a responsibility similar to that of a doctor who is pledged to keep secret the details of what may be causing the illness of a patient.

One's reading is as personal as his private hopes and fears, and must be respected accordingly. To make a P.A. of a person and then broadcast the fact that you have found the intelligence to be low and the low self bothered by fixations and giving a counter-clockwise reaction, is unthinkable and could cause considerable trouble. Also, keep in mind the fact that such a reading may be wrong. Be most circumspect. In telling what you have read, qualify it by saying, "This is how I make the reading, but keep in mind the possibility that I may be wrong."

Perhaps the responsibility more nearly fits the situation in which a priestly confessor finds himself in relation to a member of his flock. One is called upon to consider the P.A. which he has made and to do everything possible to understand and to explain its meaning. Then he must do his best to offer advice about overcoming defects which have been uncovered, or plans to make the best use of the degree of intelligence which is indicated.

The child with a reading of less than 330 degrees should be given training aimed at the trades, not at the professions. On the other hand, the subject with a reading of over 330 degrees should be directed into walks of life better suited to his degree level. A man with a reading of 370 will make a good doctor, but will be unhappy as a carpenter in all probability.

Even the best readers will at times find a person for whom they can make no reading. The pendulum either does not move or swings aimlessly. Why this happens is not yet known, but it happens. There are other people for whom one may get a different reading every time, so check and recheck.

It is manifestly impossible for the writer to attempt to check readings, so a group should be organized so that checks can be run within the group.

This is pioneer work of a high order, and anyone giving time to learning the art and forming a group will be performing a most valuable public service.

One low self seems to learn to use its psychic abilities by association with another low self which has already acquired skill. A good reader can be of great help to others who are just beginning. The one to be taught should first become familiar with the instructions given for the use of the method as well as with the theory. The meaning of the various actions of the pendulum over the chart should especially be studied and memorized, otherwise the beginner's low self will not have the absolutely necessary under-standing of what it is to look for in making the examination or how to relay that information through the use of the pendulum, code and chart.

It has been found that when one is well grounded in the theoretical side of the work, the low self is made to realize the validity and workability of it all by watching an experienced reader make readings and by hearing the explanations given of them. For such practice, the pictures of people in the news will offer an excellent variety of subjects, some good, some bad, some intelligent, and some with much "soul" evolution still ahead of them.

Another part of the basic training is that of determining whether or not the one to be read is alive or has passed on to the next stage of existence.

The code to be used here is a clockwise circle of the pendulum for the living and a counterclockwise or "negative" circle for the dead. If one is not sure whether the subject is dead or alive, one simply asks the low self at the start of the reading to investigate and show by the proper positive or negative circle what the condition may be.

As a rule, this dead-or-alive indication is given first, that is, before the regular reading comes. If one has worked a short time with the pictures or the signatures of those who have gone on, the low self will get the idea and of its own accord will begin a reading of one deceased with the negative circle. In most work of this kind one will be using reproductions of original photographs or letters bearing the signatures. If both a letter and a picture are available, it is good to make a reading from each in turn. A forged signature or letter will not give the same reading as will a picture of the supposed writer.

The low self seems in some way to be able to trace the shadowy threads from a reproduction of an original photograph with ease. In the specimen readings given in the later pages of this book will be found one made from a photograph of a sculptured bust of Abraham Lincoln. As the bust was made by the sculptor from a study of photographs, it may be seen what skill the low self develops in this "hop-skip-and-jump" method of rushing back to find the actual subject, be he in the flesh or in his shadowy body in the "hereafter".

With one's own children, the readings should be checked against similar readings made by others in your group to be sure that parental pride and judgment have not colored your own readings. Someone who hardly knows a child will probably make the best reading.

A word of warning was given by a teacher in the matter of general readings to accompany the regular I.Q. ratings of pupils. She had discovered, much to her distress, that parents were inclined to show a considerable amount of resentment if their children were described to them as less than perfect in all parts of the analysis. On the other hand, a teacher can gain a very helpful insight into the natures of her pupils by making readings from their inked signatures, and, of course, it is not necessary to tell what the readings have disclosed.

In schools, mental hospitals and reformatory institutions, one of the major difficulties has been the lack of a simple method by which individuals can be classified. In the schools the students of low intelligence are hardly distinguishable for at least a year.

Later on, when the standard I.Q. tests are made, a step toward classification can be taken, but there is still much to be done in the following grades. In the matter of classification for the better handling of the ever-troublesome problems of discipline, almost nothing is done systematically.

When a student is old enough to seek guidance in the matter of education for a future occupation, the P.A. reading would give immediate classification of the general intelligence level and attention could be turned at once to the proper training schedules. All too often, under the present system, the student has been influenced by the parents to wish to enter some particular profession for which he may seem to be intelligent enough to qualify, when, as a matter of fact, he is not quite up to the mark.

The student with a "V" will pattern should not be encouraged to enter a trade or profession where he has to direct others. He will be far happier and far more successful working under someone who will tell him what to do and take the initiative.

One whose P.A. reading shows fixations or the possible presence of spirits influencing him, should not be directed to occupations in which there may be great responsibility and strain. He will do well if he can find a nitch in which he has only himself to over-see, and only his own work to do.

In all reformatory or penal institutions the P.A. readings of those being entered would help because a reliable classification of the naturally bad and the more easily influenced individuals could be made. At present the individuals who could be reformed with proper retraining are often thrown in with the hope-lessly bad and vicious, the result too often being that the worst possible things are learned and a school for crime soon produces another graduate.

In the matter of handling criminals in prisons, each one should be given a reading at the time of his entry. Then, at any later date a check reading could be made to see whether the prisoner had changed for better or worse under the reformatory methods used.

When the prisoner had served a sufficient amount of time to come up for parole, a fresh reading could be made and checked against all former readings. If there were no signs of reform, the parole board would know immediately whether the prisoner could be released with safety or should be handled in such a way that the public would be safeguarded against a quick resumption of criminal acts.

The prisoner who stoutly affirms his innocence and who insists that he has been "framed", will be given a much better chance of having justice meted out to him if his P.A. reading can be taken and its indications noted. If his is the reading of a natural criminal, he may be judged greatly suspect.

The mentally ill have already been discussed and it has been pointed out that obsession and spirit influences can be identified easily with a reading. The doctors would be greatly helped if they could know which patients are ill because of purely physical ailments and which are suffering from fixations and obsessive invasion of the personality.

Some work has been done in this direction and much more needs to be done. But even now the obsessive patients could be separated from those who suffer from physical breakdowns of various kinds. Evidence already points to a very real danger. The spirits obsessing one patient may leave him and go to fasten himself on another, or upon some attendant who is susceptible to such influences.

An interesting possibility is that in addition to the identification of people through the use of files of fingerprints, P.A. readings can be made from them. If, out of several sets of fingerprints found at the scene of a crime, one set gave a reading such as is common to criminals, the work of the police would be much simplified.

The age of predatory freedom for the "wolf in sheep's clothing" may be drawing to an end. With the increasing use of Psychometric Analysis, the confidence man and all his ilk will become so well known for what they are that they can no longer ply their evil trades. The gangster and the crooked politician will no longer be able to pretend honesty.

In politics the intelligence and integrity of candidates for office can quickly be ascertained, and the best men given the task of making the laws and improving the tone of government.

The commercial value of the readings has already been well demonstrated. One firm found that P.A. readings of applicants for positions as salesmen in the mutual funds field saved much time. The readings made it possible to do away with the costly method of hiring men and watching them at work in order to be able to learn which ones were reliable and which were not.

The time may be closer than we think when an applicant for a position will either have his signature given a P.A test or it will be customary for all applicants to submit their readings when filing their applications.

If war should come again and a large conscript

army be called into being, the P.A. readings would weed out the mentally, emotionally and criminally unfit so that they would not be inducted, and later become a burden to be carried with public funds.

Looking forward for the "hundred years" which we have in mind when we say of a man's inventions, "He is a hundred years ahead of his time," we may envision the day when the P.A. readings, perhaps by then greatly improved, will have helped reshape the educational, economic and governmental systems of the world.

In the revolution against feudalism a few centuries ago in the Western world, the ideal of equality was based on the God-given right of every human being to inherit the same basic privileges. Democracy, which was the ideal political expression of equal rights, has been a great improvement on slavery and feudalism, but it is still a hit-or-miss system.

The ancient caste system and the variant of the class system were based on the accident of birth, and the imbecile often inherited the throne and the power that went with it. In Communist China there recently arose the threat of the formation of a class composed of those with a superior education. As no way had been planned to deal with such a class, the students were sent from the classrooms to work part of their time in the fields, factories and elsewhere. This, perhaps, might keep for them "the common touch", but we cannot escape the fact that it is a great waste of human talent to use an intelligent student to do the work of the least intelligent laborer. A better way must be found, the world over, to make the best use of the many and widely varied talents and aptitudes of men and women.

90

In the last analysis, we are suffering from a lack of effort to replace the hit-or-miss method by well planned systematization in which a place is made for each level of men, classified according to their intelligence and ability. Eventually, we will be forced by the weight of economic necessity to make fuller and better plans and to conform our lives to them.

While the problems of the world seem almost too difficult and complicated to solve, there are many encouraging signs on all sides. The sheer pressure of populations will keep alive the movements which have forced us to make atomic progress so rapidly. There is bound to be more and more thought given to human engineering as well as other types, and in due time Psychometric Analysis will come into its own, if for no other reason than that it is too valuable in too many phases of life to be overlooked.

*   *   *   *   *

The following readings will show the general way in which the chart is used for readings. A study of them will make the system clearer to the beginner.

PLEASE NOTE: On the following pages the chart faces have been reduced slightly for the sake of convenience in reproducing them and giving examples of the meanings of the readings and code symbols.

The chart face, as used in taking readings, is a full two inches in diameter.

Readers customarily record their readings on a chart face with red pencil for the "will" pattern and blue pencil for the "personality" pattern circle. The degree reading can be written at one side with black pencil or ink. The use of colors on the chart makes it easier to see the patterns, but as this book is not printed in colors, the code is added at one side.

A fresh chart slip is generally used by the reader for each test, the data being set down on the same slip. For keeping a record on file of each reading, a carbon copy can easily be made.

Abbreviations used in the following readings:
"c" or "d" in quotes denotes the circle size.
cc stands for counterclockwise.
c stands for clockwise.
ccl stands for counterclockwise leaning.
cl stands for clockwise leaning.

PLEASE NOTE: The sample readings which follow may or may not be correct.

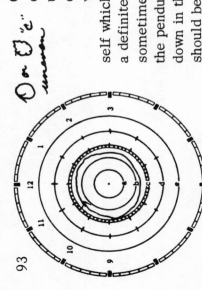

O or O "e"
uneven

Care should be taken, in making an evaluation of a reading, not to confuse an uncertain and uneven personality circle swing with a mental defect. The subject may be quite normal in all ways except for a badly worried or upset low self which does not know just what to do. A fixation of a definite sort usually flattens the circle, but worry or sometimes illness produces the uneven swing in which the pendulum seems to wobble and waver. This is set down in the record as a regular circle, but beside it should be placed the comment, "uneven", "very irreg-

ular" or "strong wobble". An uneven circle can also be drawn to show the trouble, but as circles are drawn very irregular on the chart in keeping them between the printed circles, the distinction should be made at one side for the record. The subject should be told that the low self is bothered and that it will be well to correct the worry habit or to try to change the conditions which cause the worry. Both selves should be confident and unafraid to do their best work as a team. For those who understand the ancient Huna philosophy, it may be added that the High Self is also a part of the natural team of three selves, and that it should be invited daily to work with the lower pair of selves, furnishing the invaluable guidance which in its superior wisdom it can give. Some day we may be able to find a way to read the part the High Self plays in one's life.

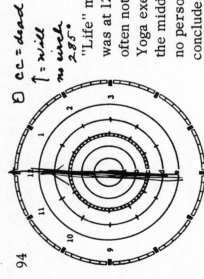

⊙ cc = dead

↑ = will

no circle

295°

Subject: Joseph Stalin, late Russian leader. Reading starts with small cc circle which indicates that the subject is dead. Reading was taken from a series of pictures reproduced in "Life" magazine. Will pattern swing as noted on chart was at 12:00 o'clock. It was the "perfect" will pattern so often noted in readings of hypnotists and "masters" of Yoga exercises involving the training of the will power of the middle self. Degree reading was 285. There was no personality circle at all - a very unusual thing. One concludes that the subject rose to power through the exercise of an amazing will power with which he could

control others. A study of his life shows no constructive ideas of his own, which fits in well with his degree reading of only 285. He appears to have accepted the Lenin teachings and to have clung to them with great fanaticism after, perhaps, simplifying them on a few points to suit his very practical purposes. Without a personality circle showing in the reading, we conclude that he was dominated entirely by his middle self. Utterly cold and calculating, he knew no softening "conscience". In a very practical way he had those who stood in his way killed, even killing masses of peasants or others who would not obey his orders. One may contrast his reading with that of his idol, Lenin, given next. This is one of the strangest readings of the many made of Russian politicians.

Subject: Nikolai Lenin (Illitch Ulyanov), a Marxian Socialist, who improved greatly the weak system proposed by Karl Marx, and whose teachings were accepted by Stalin and remained his gospel without change. Lenin had almost as strong a will as Stalin, and also had almost no sign of a personality circle. Both men believed that "the end (which they visualized as the goal of Socialism) justified the means", and that nothing was to be allowed to stand between them and their purpose. Lenin, at 378 degrees had the intelligence needed to work out the system, but

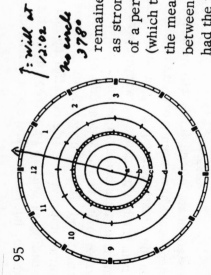

1: will at 12:02

no circle 378°

Stalin, at 285 degrees could only follow blindly. Karl Marx was not quite as intelligent as Lenin, having a reading of 374 degrees. On the other hand, Marx had a normal and constructive will and personality pattern, making him a giant of kindness and morality in comparison with the two who followed his line of thought. At the time of his death, Stalin was surrounded with henchmen, all of them with a counterclockwise personality pattern, and all with low degree readings. Georgei Malenkov was 316 degrees, Bulganin was 293, Minister of Foreign Affairs Molotov was 269, and Beria was 315. They were a set of evil and loudly vocal politicians, none capable of beginning the basic reconstruction of the revolt-torn land. Kerensky at 353, and General Brusilov at 363, tried to take over after the big revolt, but both lacked the iron will needed at the moment.

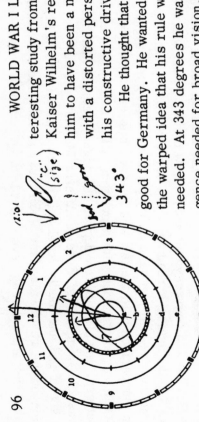

WORLD WAR I LEADERS, make a very interesting study from the point of view of P.A. Kaiser Wilhelm's reading, at the left, shows him to have been a man of powerful will, but with a distorted personality pattern, which gave his constructive drives a strange abnormality. He thought that what he wanted must be good for Germany. He wanted to rule the world, and had the warped idea that his rule would be what the world needed. At 343 degrees he was below the level of intelligence needed for broad vision. He could never have been a statesman, although his will made him a leader of outstanding ability. His military men would have been more cautious and circumspect had they been permitted to decide on the question of engaging in such a conquest. It has been noted that physical deformity from birth often causes a warped personality to match. The Kaiser was a very proud man, and his bad arm demanded mental compensations. He was driven to try to show superiority in every possible way. On the other hand, people crippled or deformed after childhood often compensate their losses in such a way that their will or personality patterns improve. A life of suffering and trouble may see a marked growth in the degree reading as well as improvement in other ways. (Helen Keller began blind, deaf and dumb, but her life and accomplishments show excellent compensation and integration.)

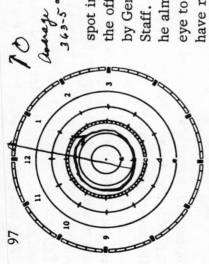

Average
363-5°

What the Kaiser started, his army and navy had to try to finish. At the left is a composite reading which shows what to look for in making a study of a military establishment. A weak spot in the Kaiser's armor was that the original plan for the offensive against Russia and France was worked out by Gen. von Falkenhayn, who also was German Chief of Staff. He had a degree reading of only 341, but in this he almost matched the Kaiser, and they must have seen eye to eye on a plan which men of broader vision could have recognized as defective. Better men had to come into the effort to salvage the plan. Gen. von Hindenburg and 363, came to the fore but had a tiny cc personality circle and was out of balance, although his will pattern was such that he made a great leader part of the time. Ludendorff gradually took the lead, becoming the real chief of staff, and 364 degrees, but he had a cc "V" pattern of will, and the crimes against humanity committed by the Germans during the war may in part be laid at his feet. His will pattern also indicates the strong leader.

Plans for naval operations were worked out by a very able man, Admiral von Tirpitz, who would have won the war for Germany had the over-all plan not been defective. His reading was and 366 degrees. He saw the value of the submarine and made use of it with telling effect, but the planned short war turned out to be too long.

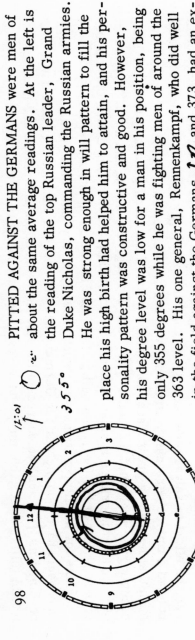

12:01 ↑ ○

355°

PITTED AGAINST THE GERMANS were men of about the same average readings. At the left is the reading of the top Russian leader, Grand Duke Nicholas, commanding the Russian armies. He was strong enough in will pattern to fill the place his high birth had helped him to attain, and his personality pattern was constructive and good. However, his degree level was low for a man in his position, being only 355 degrees while he was fighting men of around the 363 level. His one general, Rennenkampf, who did well in the field against the Germans, ↑○ and 373, had an excellent will pattern and a personality circle warp closely resembling that of the Kaiser. The Nihilists, those "angry men" who were the "Reds" of the day, had assassinated Tsar Alexander II, and his son, Nicholas II was on the uneasy throne. But Nicholas was not a leader ↑○ and 335 degrees, although he meant well and tried to make a few reforms. His cousin, George V of England ↑○ and 332, was very similar in reading and in his lack of ability. All depended on the caliber of the fighting men and the top civil leaders who stood behind them. England was fortunate in having Field Marshal Sir Douglas Haig ↑○ and 362 degrees, to lead her armies. France, unfortunately for her, had to start resisting the Germans under Field Marshal Joffre ↑○ and 345 degrees, who was a fine leader and poor planner. Marshal Foch ↑○ and 364 degrees, had to turn the tide.

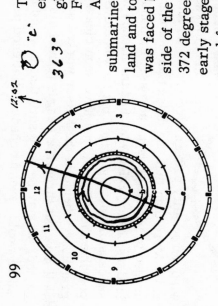

12:02

↑ ☾ "e"

363°

The defect in the German plans became apparent when the United States came into the struggle and sent General Pershing with troops to France. His reading is on the chart at the left. Admiral von Tirpitz at 366 degrees was using submarines and raiders to starve out France and England and to try to stop the flow of troops by sea. But he was faced by a more intelligent and inventive man on the side of the Allies, Admiral Sir David Beatty ↗☾ and 372 degrees, who bested him with his own forces at the early stages of the war, and with the help of the U.S.A. naval forces later on. Vice Admiral Sims, commanding for the U.S.A. in Europe ↗☾ and 345 degrees, fortunately, did not have to make plans. Over him was the Secretary of the Navy, Josephus Daniels /☾ and 365, who worked with the British hand in glove. England started her war in 1914 with her Admiral Rushworth Jellicoe at the head of her navy ↗☾ and 313 degrees, but he was no match for the clever von Tirpitz and in 1916 had to be replaced by Beatty. One can only wonder how a man of his level ever got to be an Admiral in the first place. The U.S.A. was fortunate to have as Secretary of War, Newton D. Baker /☾ and 370 degrees. Robert Lansing was Secretary of State ↗☾ and 374. They were both very able men. The French had Clemenceau ↑☾ and 365 degrees. England had Lloyd George ↗☾ and 364 degrees.

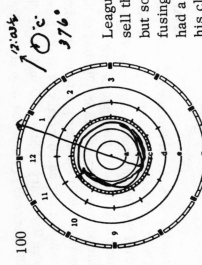

12:04½
↑O'c.
376°

Woodrow Wilson was our World War I president (see reading at left), and while men of lesser degree levels were making the peace, he was working far above their heads on a plan to prevent world wars in the future. He proposed a League of Nations, and did everything in his power to sell the idea to the world. In this he was successful, but soon the little men at home scuttled the plan by refusing to let the United States join the League. Wilson had a balanced and judicial mind, as is indicated by his clockwise leaning will pattern and good round clockwise personality pattern circle. But he lacked the "perfect" will pattern of great leaders. More than that, he did not have a man to work with him who had the will strength needed to put the League across. England's Lloyd George was one of the few civilian leaders of the period who had the needed will pattern to drive the League through to a successful working stage, but he was eleven degrees lower on the scale, and it is quite possible that he would not have seen clearly how the League was to operate. Had the grandiose scheme of the Kaiser worked out to allow him to control the world, he might well have put through a League plan of his own, for the idea was not a new one. But if he had, we may be very sure that it would have been a very warped and oppressive plan which would have matched his flattened personality circle.

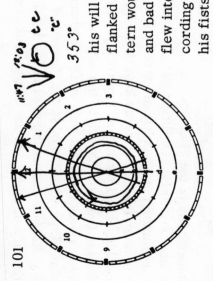

353°

Adolph Hitler (reading at left) was a most interesting study from the P.A. reading point of view. His degree level is that of the psychic who can be a medium or a fortuneteller. But his will pattern included the "perfect" pattern, although flanked by both cc and c swings. In some men this pattern would mean a powerful influence by spirits, good and bad. Hitler may have had periods of obsession. He flew into rages and foamed at the mouth at times, according to his biographers, even attacking generals with his fists. The history of his actions indicates personality changes in which he could be good or bad or neutral and hypnotically commanding. His degree number of 353 fits very well with what we know of his mentality. He had a good memory and a mind for details, but his generalizations were defective. When he forced war, it was against the judgment of the army commanders. Later, when the war was being lost, he refused to consider final defeat and became his own top strategist, making matters only worse. He was a great and unscrupulous leader who lacked the breadth of vision to look ahead realistically. Stalin's general staff advised against his desire to turn and do battle with Hitler. He purged the general staff and attacked. Hitler constantly ran counter to the advice of his general staff, but did not purge its members. Instead, they plotted long to overthrow him, and he escaped assassination by pure luck.

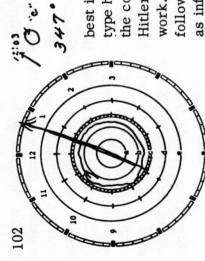

1:03
1 O'c"
347°

Heinrich Himmler, whose reading is on the left, furnishes a fine example of "the exception which proves the rule." His patterns were clockwise and must be read as those of a kindly man of the best intentions. But after the evil men of the Goering type had started the extermination of Jews and Slavs, and the confiscation of their property, with the full consent of Hitler, it fell to Himmler's lot to continue the terrible work. This he did. He was one of Hitler's blindly loyal followers, and Hitler's predictions were accepted by him as infallible. He also accepted Hitler's doctrine of the superiority of the "Nordics" and the necessity of cleansing the earth of races which had contaminated it. To Hitler this doctrine was used or set aside as he found expedient, but for Himmler it was ultimate truth. In this respect he must be recognized as a complete and utter fanatic. He was kind to his inferiors and they loved him. He gave the orders, but left actual torture and murder to others. He resembled the kindly bishops of the Roman Catholic Church in the days of the Inquisition. Many are recorded in history as very kindly men, but they were convinced that it was better to torture and kill rather than allow a soul to miss the chance for salvation. Himmler actually thought he was doing the only proper thing. His low level of degree reading fits his accomplishments or, the lack of them. At the last he took over an army and proved a very poor commander.

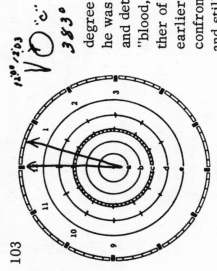

Franklin D. Roosevelt (see chart) was the president of the United States when Hitler started out to try to realize a dream which was wilder by far than that of the Kaiser. This time the degree level of the German leader was a bit higher, but he was faced by two men of most unusual intelligence and determination, F.D.R. and Winston Churchill of "blood, sweat and tears". (His reading: **VOS83**) Neither of these mature men had owned the perfect will in earlier years. They rose to meet the emergencies that confronted them, developed the needed strength of will, and still kept the old will pattern slant which marks the man who is flexible and who can change enough to be an expert politician. France, sad to say, had been struck by Hitler at a time when she was without able leadership. The Maginot Line was useless. The feeble resistance crumpled, allowing the British to be driven into the sea. Hitler had been acting on his hunches rather than on the advice of the general staff of his time. The success of attempts which had the elements of being things insane to try, encouraged him to even more rash endeavors. But his luck could not hold, and his daring was mixed with indecision. The Allies gradually built up power and went over to the attack. General Eisenhower and General George Marshall, both fully clockwise and with outstandingly high degree readings took hold. Exit Hitler.

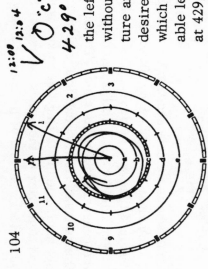

Having mentioned presidents and their readings in the foregoing pages, this will be a good time to see what makes a famous president from the point of view of the P.A. tests. On the chart at the left is the reading for George Washington, taken not without some difficulty from reproductions of his signature and painted portraits. His will pattern shows the desired combination of perfect will and flexible will which we have come to associate with men of unusually able leadership and political skill. His degree reading at 429, if this is correct, would make him the highest

of any president tested. Abraham Lincoln $V\mathcal{O}$ and 425 degrees, had almost the same reading, and we know what vision they had in playing their parts in the formation of the nation and its preservation. Both men were fully clockwise and so, fully good and constructive. Neither one wavered in driving at all costs toward the ends which to them appeared to be best for the nation and the time. Both were very kind and sympathetic.

From studies of the will pattern (such as we have seen in readings of these men of greatness), it is to be concluded that it is possible to strengthen one's will by making a great and prolonged effort. Hypnotists appear to develop the perfect will pattern ($\updownarrow$) by learning intense concentration and endeavor to influence their subjects mentally. The practice of Yoga seems also to produce the same result.

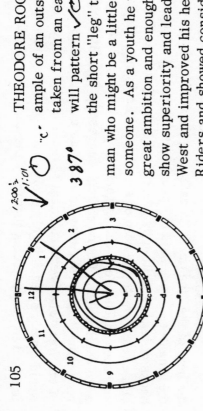

12:00
V "c"

387°

THEODORE ROOSEVELT (at left) offers an example of an outstanding president. A reading taken from an early photograph gave for the will pattern ⟲. This was rather weak and the short "leg" to the cc side would fit a salesman who might be a little unscrupulous in over-selling someone. As a youth he was not too strong, but he had great ambition and enough egotism to make him wish to show superiority and leadership. He roughed it in the West and improved his health. He organized the Rough Riders and showed considerable leadership. He developed an outward strut-and-swagger attitude and managed to sell himself sufficiently in political circles to get the position of vice president. He was a colorful figure and adept at keeping in the public eye. He was elected president. His intelligence, developed will power and flexible skill in politics made for some larger accomplishments. But behind the rough-and-ready front which he carefully built up with hunting trips and similar exploits, there was a touch of the "professor". He was an excellent student, and he came to write clearly and with an easy style. He was no mean naturalist, but found no great recognition for his talents and writings on that line. He drew attention by attacking the "nature fakers". Building on the work of other men, he proclaimed a system of simplified spelling. He took the floor, held it, and tried very hard to deserve to hold it.

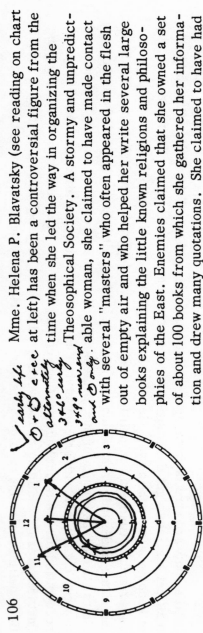

Early life
Org cree
alimitary
346 only
349 never end
and only.

Mme. Helena P. Blavatsky (see reading on chart at left) has been a controversial figure from the time when she led the way in organizing the Theosophical Society. A stormy and unpredictable woman, she claimed to have made contact with several "masters" who often appeared in the flesh out of empty air and who helped her write several large books explaining the little known religions and philosophies of the East. Enemies claimed that she owned a set of about 100 books from which she gathered her information and drew many quotations. She claimed to have had the help of the "masters" in gathering the material and writing about it. For some years the "masters" were said to "precipitate" letters to various Theosophists, often on the backs of letters written by others and already in transit. She was accused of faking some of the letters with the help of servants while living in India. These letters have been reproduced in Theosophical journals and in books. Readings of the signatures of the letters were duplications of her reading, suggesting that either she wrote them or, that, if written by the "masters", they used her as a medium in some way as the characteristics of the "masters" were identical to those of H.P.B. As her reading was not such as one would expect by such highly evolved and perfected men as the "mahatmas", more doubt is added to the suspicion that the "masters" were only ordinary spirits (see Pg. 108.)

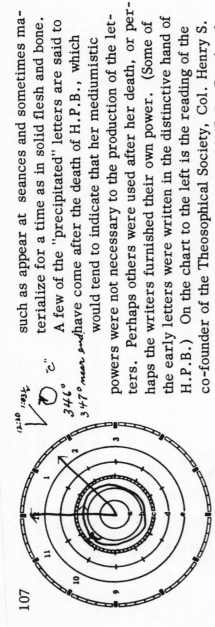

H.P.B.'s

346°

347° mean and

such as appear at seances and sometimes ma-
terialize for a time as in solid flesh and bone.
A few of the "precipitated" letters are said to
have come after the death of H.P.B., which
would tend to indicate that her mediumistic
powers were not necessary to the production of the letters. Perhaps others were used after her death, or perhaps the writers furnished their own power. (Some of
the early letters were written in the distinctive hand of
H.P.B.) On the chart to the left is the reading of the
co-founder of the Theosophical Society, Col. Henry S.

Olcott, who had a degree reading even lower than the low reading of H.P.B. People of
this level are often mediumistic, and are often used by spirits, but seldom construct for
the world a set of plans such as Lenin produced for the revolutionists of his day, or such
as Woodrow Wilson produced for the League of Nations. The writings of H.P.B. were of
a grade so high as to suggest a more intelligent author. Were these "masters"? Later
on, Annie Besant ∨ and 377 degrees, and C. W. Leadbeater ∨ and 367 degrees did
excellent work in writings to explain what H.P.B. had set down in a difficult-to-follow
style. Oddly enough, the "masters" failed to see weakness in some T.S. associates,
and the instructions and advice given through the letters often fell far short of what one
would expect of "masters". In any event, the T.S. was formed and is still at work.

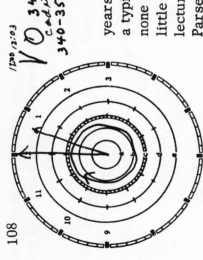

108

While the question of the validity of "masters" and of their superior powers and intelligence remains yet to be answered, we do have some readings (taken from pictures) of several "holy men" who have lived in India in the past hundred years. At the left has been charted what may be called a typical reading for the best of them. They vary almost none at all in will and personality patterns, and only a little in degree. Egypt's famous Yoga practitioner and lecturer (Arab), Dr. Tahra Bey $V\bigcirc$ and 343. In India: Parsee, Meher Baba, who has a world-wide following and who promises to break his vocal silence one day and bring a new day to the world as he speaks, $V\bigcirc$ 347. Shri Shankara, described by Paul Brunton as "the spiritual head of South India, $V\bigcirc$ 338. The "master", Mahasaya, one of the famous Ramakrishna's chelas, $V\bigcirc$ 346. Sarada Devi, "The Holy Mother", wife of Ramakrishna, $V\bigcirc$ 341. Sahabji Maharaj, "Master of over one hundred thousand people who practice a mysterious form of Yoga", (Brunton in his "A Search in Secret India") $V\bigcirc$ 351. "The Maharishee or Great Sage", $V\bigcirc$ 346. Pictures of six modern gurus or spiritual teachers, given by W. Y. Evans-Wentz in his book, "Tibetan Yoga and Secret Doctrines", give the standard patterns for such men and the highest degree noted was 343. One must decide that one can be both holy and wise, and read well below 350.

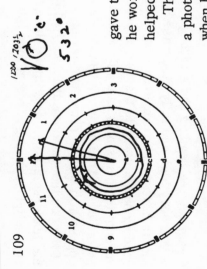

It has been possible to get readings from only two Polynesian native priests or kahunas. And even then the reading of the one in spirit from Samoa, $\sqrt{}$ ○ and 554 degrees, "Hoola" (to cause life, is the meaning of the name which he gave to Jessie Curl, the English medium through whom he works) had to be made from a drawing which he helped the psychic artist, Frank Leah, to execute.

The other reading (see chart at left) was made from a photograph of a native "keeper of the Secret" taken when he was a very old man. His name is not known, but he was reputed to be a famous healer and remarkable psychic, able to see and to drive away spirits who were causing the living trouble. In the work of the Huna Research Associates, efforts were made to develop similar white kahunas, but in no case was anyone found of such a high degree reading. At 550 the "higher form of intuition" was said by Dr. Brunler to be found, in contrast to the lower form common to mediums and other "sensitives" at the 340-350 level. Slow healing using the "lesser magic" is possible with those of readings as low as 260 degrees, but instant healing through the natural powers inherited by the 550 degree level people, seem reserved for those who are willing to learn to use the "high magic", which is part of the lore of the ancient Huna system which was preserved in Polynesia for so many centuries.

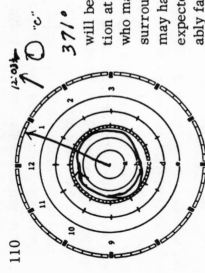

Some day in the future, P.A. readings will be made of every public figure whose character may influence relations between nations or the lives of those of their own nation. No diplomat will be without a list of such readings. The world situation at the present writing is in the hands of strong men who may have the power of dictators. These are always surrounded by lesser associates. In predicting what may happen, the readings will help to tell who is to be expected to accomplish good things and who will probably fail in his ventures if opposed by someone with a higher degree reading and a stronger will pattern. Of course, as we have seen, a man with a very high and fully clockwise reading may have fanatical beliefs which will cause him to have peculiar or even very dangerous ideas of what is good and what is bad. The reading on the chart is that of the present leader of Russia, Khrushchev. His reforms and accomplishments bear out well what his reading suggests. If he is not too fanatical in his hatred of the free nations, he may do much to ease the conflicts of the "cold war". We oppose him with a president having a far higher degree reading and so a far wider view of the tangled world conditions. Had Khrushchev possessed a more perfect will pattern, his leadership might have made things easier by far for him to realize his ambitions. He is a delightful change from a long line of counterclockwise and low degree Red leaders.

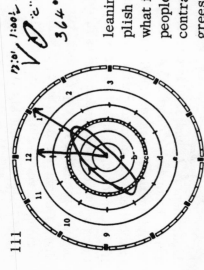

The reading for China's Mao Tse-Tung is at the left. He has the will pattern of the ideal leader. He is of good degree level, but his personality pattern shows in the flattened clockwise circle with its axis following the leaning leg of his will pattern. While he tries to accomplish only good for his people, his warped idea of just what is good will have run counter to those of the many people over whom he came to have rigid authority. In contrast we have Chiang Kai-shek ∨Ð∵ and 346 degrees, who meant well, being clockwise in personality pattern, but who had a weak will pattern which made him lack decision and threw him open to the evil influence of others. Mao is reported to have chosen a successor, Liu Shao-chi ∨Ð∵ and 372 degrees, who, from his good reading, promises to have a much more balanced view, and who might be very good for Red China and easier for the West to deal with. The Dalai Lama, recently forced from power in Tibet by the Chinese ∕Ð∵ and 289 degrees, would appear not to have a chance to lead the people, some of whom look upon him as a reincarnation of the Buddha. Mme. Chiang Kai-shek's reading makes an interesting study, ∨Ð and 362 degrees. It is to be guessed that she has been the power behind the throne all these years and has perhaps been responsible for some of the General's less praiseworthy actions when in China proper.

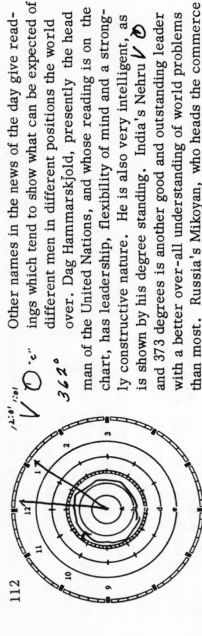

Other names in the news of the day give readings which tend to show what can be expected of different men in different positions the world over. Dag Hammarskjöld, presently the head man of the United Nations, and whose reading is on the chart, has leadership, flexibility of mind and a strongly constructive nature. He is also very intelligent, as is shown by his degree standing. India's Nehru and 373 degrees is another good and outstanding leader with a better over-all understanding of world problems than most. Russia's Mikoyan, who heads the commerce department and 376, is constructive and possibly a friend of the West. On the other hand, Gromyko and 363 degrees, will continue to be a difficult man to work with in diplomatic exchanges. His will pattern indicates that he will be stubborn in holding to a belief, but changing with each wind which blows from those in authority above him. Christian Herter and 366 degrees, appears to be a determined leader and is fully constructive. De Gaulle of France and 363 degrees is also a very good man but may be too inflexible for the good of his administration. Germany's Adenauer and 372 degrees, may have to let go because of his age although a very valuable man. Willy Brandt, mayor of West Berlin, is a good man and 367 degrees, but his will pattern does not show the great leader.

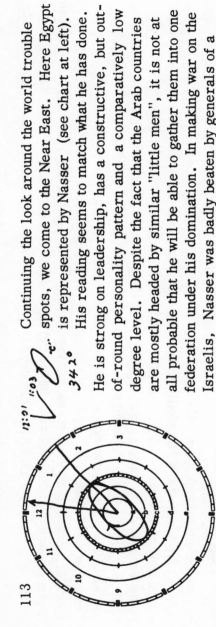

Continuing the look around the world trouble spots, we come to the Near East. Here Egypt is represented by Nasser (see chart at left).

His reading seems to match what he has done. He is strong on leadership, has a constructive, but out-of-round personality pattern and a comparatively low degree level. Despite the fact that the Arab countries are mostly headed by similar "little men", it is not at all probable that he will be able to gather them into one federation under his domination. In making war on the Israelis, Nasser was badly beaten by generals of a much higher degree level. General Kassem, who headed a revolt in Iraq in which King Faisal was killed has a reading of / and 352 degrees. The Middle East as well as the Near East will probably continue to boil, but as yet no leader has appeared with a reading which would suggest that he might make a single unit of these lands. Africa will also be a land of revolts and makeshift attempts to establish democratic rule. Readings on several native leaders run from 309 to 356 degrees. Jomo Kenyatta, leader of the Mau Maus reads but 325 degrees. Ghana's Kawame Nkrumah / and 334, is about aver-age, but that is not enough. And still, a negro leader may one day appear who will fill the need. Intelligence and leadership are not confined to the lighter-skinned races. A Ralph Bunch might be able to do wonders in Africa.

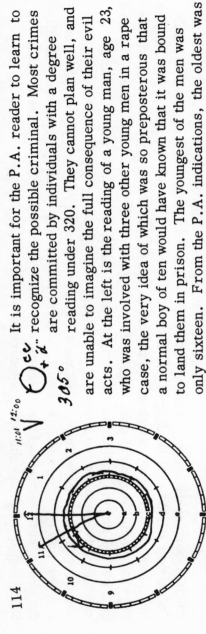

It is important for the P.A. reader to learn to recognize the possible criminal. Most crimes are committed by individuals with a degree reading under 320. They cannot plan well, and are unable to imagine the full consequence of their evil acts. At the left is the reading of a young man, age 23, who was involved with three other young men in a rape case, the very idea of which was so preposterous that a normal boy of ten would have known that it was bound to land them in prison. The youngest of the men was only sixteen. From the P.A. indications, the oldest was undoubtedly the ringleader. He alone had the will pattern of a leader. The other three showed the V pattern of the easily influenced, and they were made even more open to the evil influence because they had counterclockwise personality or low self patterns. One had a warped and changing cc circle, indicating that he might be subject to obsession at times. Here are the readings of the three who were led: V 267, V 283, V 272. These are serious defects. Less serious trouble is caused when the "house is divided against itself" by having the middle self clockwise while the low self is counterclockwise, or vice-versa, giving readings such as these /O or \O. This can happen at any degree level and causes the individual to be inwardly at war, subject to changing moods and unaccountable days of good deeds alternating with days of bad deeds.

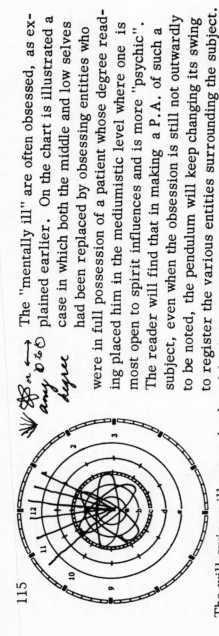

The "mentally ill" are often obsessed, as explained earlier. On the chart is illustrated a case in which both the middle and low selves had been replaced by obsessing entities who were in full possession of a patient whose degree reading placed him in the mediumistic level where one is most open to spirit influences and is more "psychic".

The reader will find that in making a P.A. of such a subject, even when the obsession is still not outwardly to be noted, the pendulum will keep changing its swing to register the various entities surrounding the subject.

The will swing will weave back and forth from side to side on the chart, while the circle will change axis or reverse from clockwise to counterclockwise. In some subjects one part of the pattern reading may be entirely missing, showing that either the middle or the low self has been prevented from functioning. This condition can be brought about, it would seem, by invading entities who bring with them the memories of illness in which the body or mind could not be used. Physical causes, especially in the aged, may make it impossible for the middle self to use the will and guide the low self. Without the normal guidance, the low self may sink into a state of inactivity...... Now and then a P.A. reading of an apparently normal person will give no circle or simply a straight line. The will swing may sometimes be down near 3:00 o'clock. Suspect trouble ahead.

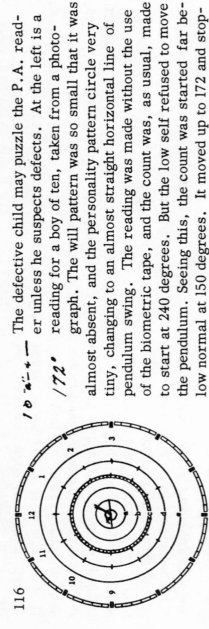

10 "=+

/ 72°

The defective child may puzzle the P. A. reader unless he suspects defects. At the left is a reading for a boy of ten, taken from a photograph. The will pattern was so small that it was almost absent, and the personality pattern circle very tiny, changing to an almost straight horizontal line of pendulum swing. The reading was made without the use of the biometric tape, and the count was, as usual, made to start at 240 degrees. But the low self refused to move the pendulum. Seeing this, the count was started far below normal at 150 degrees. It moved up to 172 and stopped, showing the fact that the boy was too far below the mental threshold to be reached by teaching. The reading, such as it is, reveals a basically constructive child who can respond to love and who will be good rather than bad according to his dim light.

A similar reading was taken from the photograph of a boy of about six. It was known that this lad was defective and the reading was simple. It was / and 211 degrees. The will swing was strong and clockwise, showing this child to be determinedly good, but there was only a blank in the reading for the low self, just a short straight swing. The indication of a defect largely lodged in the low self mind, and if it is defective, learning is very difficult. Memory is the chief active ability of the low self mind. This active and determined child will be much harder to control than the other.

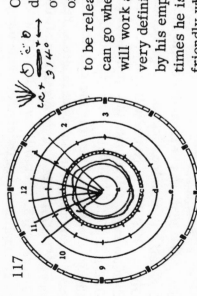

On the chart at the left is the reading of an in-dividual who appears to be obsessionally taken over by spirits only at times. He can pass all of the tests for sanity, seemingly when wishing to be released from an institution. When released, he can go where he is not known and soon find a job. He will work at it steadily for a time, then begin to show very definite signs of mental illness. He is discharged by his employer and soon is back in an institution. At times he is vindictive and bad, but often is kind and very friendly when in hospitals. From the changing of the place or strongly influence both his middle and low self. His normal reading, when not obsessed seems to be ∨ ☾ and it is important to note that he has a cc circle, making him naturally bad and prone to attract bad spirits to him and respond to their urges to be evil. His will pattern, a V, makes him naturally subject to the influence of others. With his degree reading of 314, he is in a level where we find many criminals, and while he has, so far, committed no major crime, he could, under certain circumstances do so.

Some day every mental hospital will have its patients given a P.A. reading when treatment begins, and again before they are released. The potentially dangerous will be released only under careful supervision or kept where they can be watched.

will swings and also of the personality circle, it is to be suspected that spirits either re-

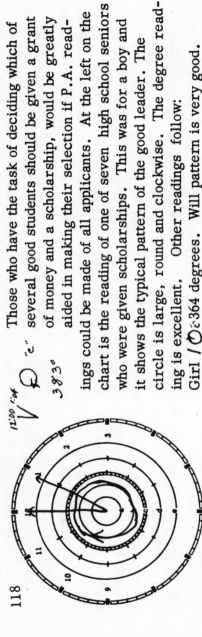

Those who have the task of deciding which of several good students should be given a grant of money and a scholarship, would be greatly aided in making their selection if P.A. readings could be made of all applicants. At the left on the chart is the reading of one of seven high school seniors who were given scholarships. This was for a boy and it shows the typical pattern of the good leader. The circle is large, round and clockwise. The degree reading is excellent. Other readings follow:

Girl / ☉¿ 364 degrees. Will pattern is very good.

Boy / ☽¿ 363. His personality circle wavered in the reading. Something bothering his low self. Best to look into the cause of this worry before awarding a scholarship.

Girl / ☉¿389. Here the will and personality pattern are good and the degree higher than average, falling into the "professor level". Here is university teacher material.

Girl /☽¿ 373. The will is strong, but the personality circle is slightly flattened although clockwise. Here is the indication of a slight defect in the low self. The girl may have been brought up in some fanatical religious belief. Best to check her carefully.

Boy /☉¿374. His is a good reading all the way through. Normal will. Good balance.

Girl/� "¼"373. Her will swing is very long and strong. It is out of proportion to the very small personality circle. Something wrong here. Best to check physical condition.

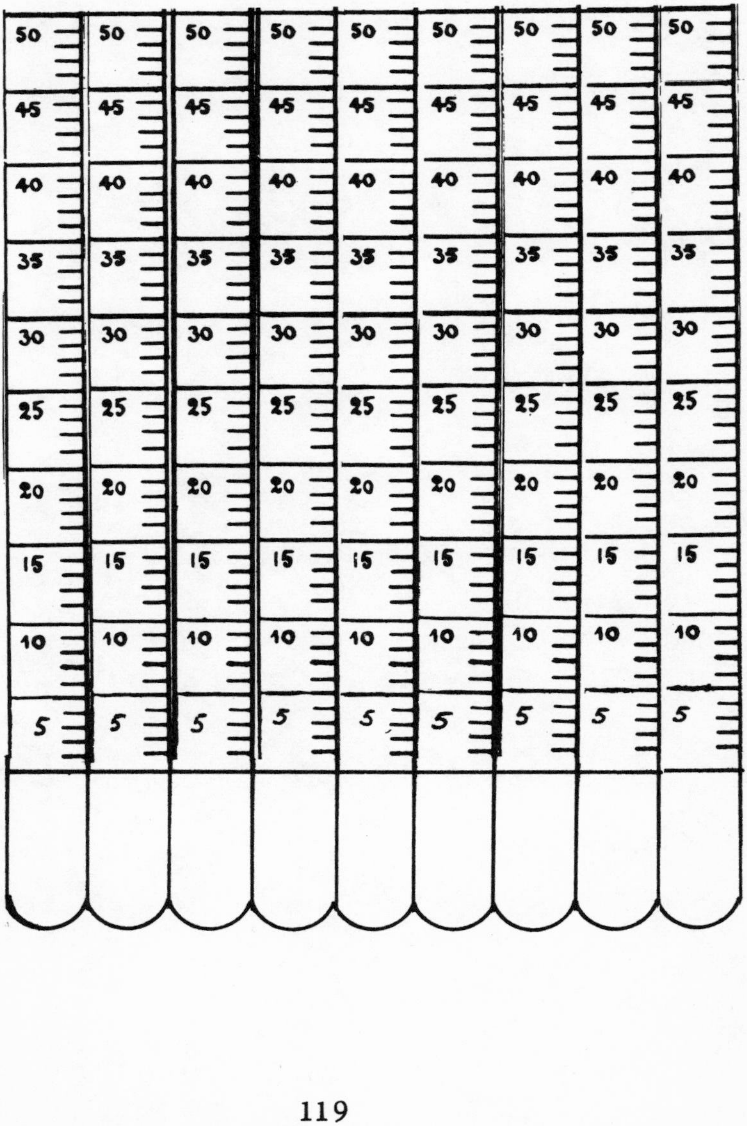
50
45
40
35
30
25
20
15
10
5

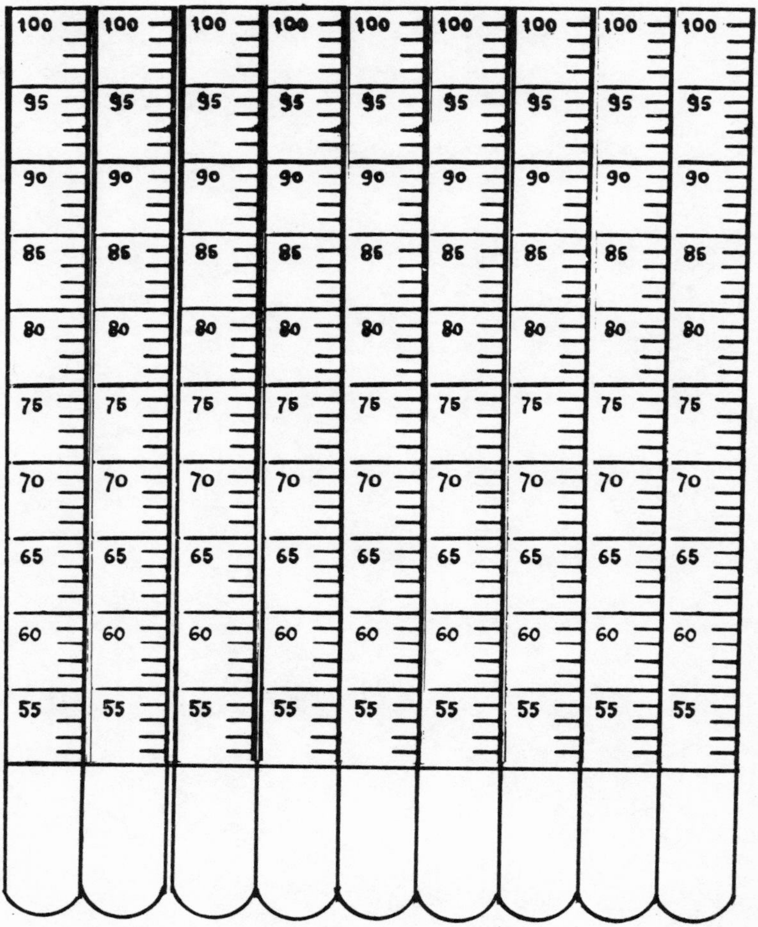
100
95
90
85
80
75
70
65
60
55

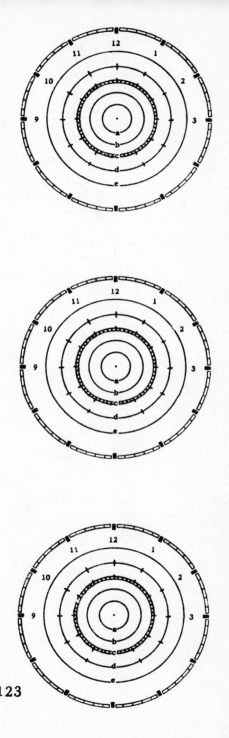

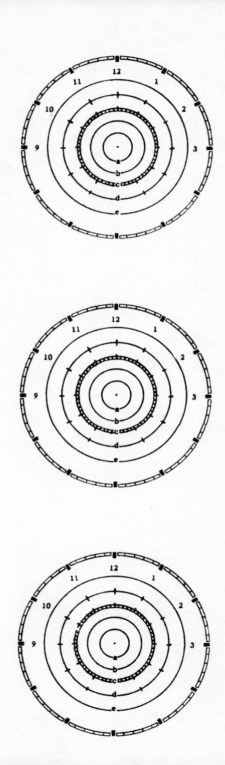